Praise for
Known

"Most of us don't get a how-to course in building lasting friendships; often we are left to figure it out as we grow up. Reading *Known* gave me a fresh look on friendship and its important role in my life. This fantastic resource of poems and stories from the Foths' personal experiences will bring incredible meaning and longevity to your relationships."

—BETSY MILLER, director, StoryBrand Foundation

"I've been learning about extravagant love from Dick and Ruth Foth for over a decade. I asked Dick if he would come with me to a country in the middle of a civil war. He said 'yes' without skipping a beat. This is how the Foths are wired. They don't see opportunities and faith and friends as separate parts of their lives but as inseparable ones. They don't love people after they've 'arrived'; they love their friends on the way. This is exactly what Jesus did. You're going to enjoy in these pages learning about friendships from the people who have been teaching me most of what I know about them."

—BOB GOFF, chief balloon inflator and author of *Love Does*

"I found myself nodding ~~~~~~~~~~~~ of *Known*. Read this book if you wa~~~~~~~~~~~~~ Read this book if you want deeper ~~~~~~~~~~~~ u want to be moved. Read this book ~~~~~~~~~~~ leaning into relationships the way Jesus intended them to be."

—BARRY H. COREY, president of Biola University and
   author of *Love Kindness: Discover the Power of a
   Forgotten Christian Virtue*

"I was twenty-eight when I got married. Standing beside me was a sixty-eight-year-old groomsman named Dick Foth. My friend. The stories and ideas captured in this book have been transforming lives through Dick and Ruth for decades. I've seen these pages in action. They have shaped my life, my family, my friends, and my community. I trust they will shape yours too."

—JEREMY VALLERAND, president and CEO,

Rescue:Freedom International

"The world is full of STORYTELLERS but starving for SAGES. When Dick and Ruth Foth write a book, we get the rare privilege of both! From Dick's anecdotes, to Ruth's poetry (and everything in between), this book is proof of the ancient truth that two are better than one! When I finished this book, I felt a renewed sense of beauty and awe for the God I serve and the people around me."

—CHAD BRUEGMAN, teaching pastor and directional

leadership, Red Rocks Church, Denver

"I look for three things from an author: credibility, authenticity, and clarity of message. Dick and Ruth Foth have delivered on all three. *Known: Finding Deep Friendships in a Shallow World is* a masterpiece! I will never look at relationships the same way again."

—HAL DONALDSON, president, Convoy of Hope

"Dick and Ruth's intensely practical yet otherworldly words will reach through the pages and gently beckon you to follow them into the deep warmth of relationships that nurture, heal, and equip you to live your dreams and fulfill your destiny."

—DAYNA BOWEN MATTHEW, author of *Just Medicine:*

A Cure for Racial Inequality in American Health Care

Finding Deep Friendships in a Shallow World

KNOWN

Dick and Ruth Foth

Foreword by Mark Batterson

WATERBROOK

Known

All Scripture quotations, unless otherwise indicated, are taken from the Holy Bible, New International Version®, NIV®. Copyright © 1973, 1978, 1984 by Biblica Inc.® Used by permission. All rights reserved worldwide. Scripture quotations marked (ESV) are taken from the ESV® Bible (the Holy Bible, English Standard Version®), copyright © 2001 by Crossway, a publishing ministry of Good News Publishers. Used by permission. All rights reserved. Scripture quotations marked (MSG) are taken from The Message. Copyright © by Eugene H. Peterson 1993, 1994, 1995, 1996, 2000, 2001, 2002. Used by permission of Tyndale House Publishers Inc. Scripture quotations marked (NKJV) are taken from the New King James Version®. Copyright © 1982 by Thomas Nelson Inc. Used by permission. All rights reserved. Scripture quotations marked (NLT) are taken from the Holy Bible, New Living Translation, copyright © 1996, 2004, 2007, 2013, 2015 by Tyndale House Foundation. Used by permission of Tyndale House Publishers Inc., Carol Stream, Illinois 60188. All rights reserved.

Italics in Scripture quotations reflect the author's added emphasis.

Trade Paperback ISBN 978-0-7352-8975-8
eBook ISBN 978-0-7352-8976-5

Copyright © 2017 by Richard Foth and Ruth Foth

Cover design by Kelly L. Howard

Published in the United States by WaterBrook, an imprint of the Crown Publishing Group, a division of Penguin Random House LLC, New York.

WATERBROOK® and its deer colophon are registered trademarks of Penguin Random House LLC.

The Cataloging-in-Publication Data is on file with the Library of Congress.

Printed in the United States of America
2017—First Edition

10 9 8 7 6 5 4 3 2 1

SPECIAL SALES
Most WaterBrook books are available at special quantity discounts when purchased in bulk by corporations, organizations, and special-interest groups. Custom imprinting or excerpting can also be done to fit special needs. For information, please e-mail specialmarketscms@penguin randomhouse.com or call 1-800-603-7051.

We write this book for twenty-two reasons:
Our four children and their spouses, who know us best, and their children, who enrich our lives at every turn with their love and their friendship.
Here's to you!
Erica and Van with *Aly* and Zach, *Claire* and David, *Sam,* and *Hope.*
Jenny and Brett with *Drew* and *Lily Grace.*
Susanna and Scott with *Jack, Will,* and *Addie.*
Chris and Traci with *Cameron, Chloe,* and *Noah.*

Contents

AFFIRMERS

Hearing Your Story,
I Learn How to Love You

COVENANTERS

In a Throwaway Culture, Staying
the Course Stands Out

DREAMERS

Dreams Fuel Hope

Foreword

I f you gave me a word association test and said, "Relationships," my immediate response would be, "Dick Foth." I've never met anyone who does relationships better! And I've been the beneficiary of that fact for two decades now. Of course, it takes two to tango. And one of the beautiful things about this book is that we don't just get Dick's viewpoint; we also get Ruth's reflections! And trust me, when Ruth speaks you want to listen very closely, very carefully! There is a raw honesty and profound dimensionality to this book because it's two-part harmony.

When I was a rookie pastor trying to find my way in ministry and in marriage, Dick Foth befriended me. Dick and Ruth invited Lora and me over to their home for our first Thanksgiving in Washington, DC. When Ruth served up a warm berry cobbler for dessert, I knew it was a friendship that needed to be cultivated!

Dick Foth has been a spiritual father to me for more than two decades now. He's been a sounding board for difficult decisions. He's offered encouraging words during tough times. And he's not afraid to ask the tough questions! In fact, he rarely asks me how I'm doing. He usually asks me how my wife and children are doing! Dick knows that it's our relationships with those who are closest to us that is the best barometer of how we're doing personally!

Simply put, there isn't anyone I've learned more from than Dick
Foth. And you're about to discover why I love and honor Dick and
Ruth so much. This book is pure gold—gold that has been refined by
seventy-five trips around the sun and fifty years of marriage. You'll
find a few theories in this book, but those theories are backed up by
hard-earned, down-to-earth lessons about life, love, and catching
tadpoles!

Dick and Ruth now live near Fort Collins, Colorado, but Dick
graciously returns to Washington, DC, to speak at National Community Church several times a year. Every time I announce that he's
coming, our church gives him an ovation. For the record, they don't
clap for anyone else, including me! Our congregation is very young—
about half are twentysomethings—and my theory is that Dick is the
grandfather they always wish they had. You'll feel the same way about
Dick and Ruth just a few pages into this book.

Dick is one of my favorite communicators, one of the best communicators on the planet. He can tell a story like nobody's business.
But after listening to his preaching for more than twenty years now, I
think I know his secret sauce. No matter what text he's speaking on,
no matter what context he's speaking in, he has a reassuring message
that comes through calm and clear: *it's going to be okay!*

Dick and Ruth have weathered some storms, including the di-
vorce of Dick's parents. They've walked through their fair share of
tough times as husband and wife, father and mother. And they've been
good old-fashioned friends to so many people during Dick's tenure as
pastor, college president, and friend to some of the most powerful
people in politics during their years in Washington, DC. But through

thick and thin, despite all the ups and downs, they're still standing. And not just standing, smiling!

The sad reality is that we live in a very shallow world, but if anyone can help you build deep friendships, it's Dick and Ruth Foth. Whether it's overcoming the aches and pains of loneliness or taking your friendships to a deeper place, you've come to the right place.

A book is a two-way street. The authors invite you into their lives, and you get to discover a whole new world. I think you'll love Dick and Ruth's world. But the reader also invites the authors into their world. I believe your life will be better because of it. I know mine has been forever imprinted, forever impacted.

—Mark Batterson

Introduction

What Really Matters

Words are easy, like the wind;
Faithful friends are hard to find.

—William Shakespeare, *The Passionate Pilgrim*

The question I asked the university student was casual.

"What's a word that you'd use to describe your generation?"

He said, "Overwhelmed!"

I said, "What do you mean? What are you overwhelmed by?"

When I heard *overwhelmed,* I saw my parents—born in 1910 and 1913 respectively—who lived through World War I, the influenza epidemic of 1917–18, the Great Depression of the 1930s, and World War II.

"Information," he said. "My generation is overwhelmed by information."

When he said *information,* two facts I had recently seen popped into my head: Children born in the 1990s belong to the first generation in the history of the world that

▌ do not have to go to an authority figure for information,[1]

   and,

▌ will be able to access more new information that will be
generated this year than in the previous five thousand
years combined![2]

"But you're so connected to each other," I continued.

He said, "Oh, yes! I'm connected to several dozen people through
Facebook and Twitter. I just don't know how to start a conversation."

His words jarred me. For me, face-to-face conversation is the stuff
of life. My thoughts zipped to Penn Station in New York City ten years
earlier. Ruth and I were sitting in a hole-in-the-wall Pizza Hut waiting
for our train to Washington, DC. An older woman approached our
table and asked if she could join us because seating was scarce. "Absolutely," we said.

As we talked, she told us of graduating from a major midwestern
university as a young woman and going to work for Hallmark in their
creative department. She rose to the executive ranks in marketing,
where she spent the rest of her career and from which she retired.
When we asked, "What brought you to New York?" she said that she
had been talked into coming out of retirement two years earlier to join
the marketing department of a large New York company.

When I asked, "What's the biggest difference in the workplace
now for you?" she replied, "It bothers me when a young person sends
me an e-mail on a subject, while sitting five feet away in the next cu-
bicle." "Why does that matter?" I asked. "It's efficient." She got quiet
for a moment, then looked straight at us and said, "I miss the face-to-
face, the eye contact. Eye contact makes us human." I doubt that she
had read the work of Atsushi Senju, a cognitive neuroscientist, who
says, "A richer mode of communication is possible right after making

eye contact. It amplifies your ability to compute all the signals so you are able to read the other person's brain."[3]

The older woman wasn't making a scientific statement. She was making a visceral statement. Just like my young university friend.

When the young man said, *"Overwhelmed"* and *"I don't know how to start a conversation,"* it was a Penn Station echo. Intrigued, I listened. And he schooled me. He had good reason to feel overwhelmed. Come to think of it, I feel that way myself half the time. The Niagara of information we have access to can drown us. How we keep up, sort through, choose, and prioritize can paralyze us. Instant access has changed everything: education, sports, business, politics, and of course, shopping!

Still, nothing has changed more than the way we talk to each other.

Communication is the name of the game. Our brains are Exhibit One. A communication marvel, the brain automatically sends and receives millions of messages a day throughout our bodies. Person-to-person communication, on the other hand, takes intent. Every arena of life—business, sports, medicine, education, the military, and families, to name a few—work only as well as we communicate. Why? Because great communication creates relationship, and relationship drives our whole lives.

At stake in this new reality, where we have keyboard control over what we wish others to know about us, is the depth of the relationships we want to build. We have all kinds of relationships, but apart from family, none is more meaningful than a friendship. Friendship, by definition, is unique. It's about investment and vulnerability. So trying to make a friend at light speed is brutal. On the Internet, I can give you *information,* but it's hard to give you *me.* That process does not happen at the tap of a key.

How then do relationships get started? What nurtures them? When God says, "It is not good that man should be alone," we know he's not kidding. Because we know alone. How do we get beyond that reality? What do we need to understand to create any kind of connection, let alone a friendship?

Glance with us for a moment in the rearview mirror. How do kids make friends? When we are young, we develop friendships on the fly. Mostly, they come from play. When I was young, I lived to play. Looking back, play set the stage for my first friendship.

My parents moved from Oakland, California, to south India when I was three years old. The next five years framed how I see the world to this day. But the year we returned to the States framed how I see *friendship.* We came to Springfield, Missouri, in the summer of 1950. The Blue Mountains of southwest India were as different from the Ozark Mountains of southwest Missouri as curried chicken was from biscuits and gravy.

It was there that I got my first bike, a bright red Schwinn. That bike became my ticket to a world of Royal Crown Colas and Eskimo Pies saturated in Ozark accents and open-door hospitality. Those were good times. And John David made them better.

John David lived three doors up from us on Williams Street on the north edge of Springfield. Born within two months of each other in the spring of 1942, he and I had *chemistry.* Whatever that means, we had it. We were Marco Polos on bikes, racing through the nearby local zoo and county fairgrounds, ranging out, when time and parents allowed, to Doling Park and the James River.

We only lived in Springfield one year, but that year was filled with fishing and hiking and spelunking through caves. The days were riddled with BB gun wars, wrestling matches, and games of every kind. The greater the challenge meant the greater the fun.

When we explored Doling Park Lake that spring, we found the tepid water at the lake's edge to be a perfect hatching site for tadpoles. Hundreds of tadpoles. Huge tadpoles. Tadpoles with oversized heads and sweeping tails. We became hunters. They became the hunted. Armed with Folgers coffee cans nailed to scrap-furring strips, we captured a bunch of those denizens of the shallows.

We took them back to the unfinished concrete basement of the Foth house and put them in a galvanized washtub. I don't remember what we fed them or how many survived the trauma. All I remember is being amazed when tails fell off and legs grew. In a few weeks, on a humid June night, the full-throated baritone songs of their cousins back at the lake filled the darkness. And we knew that something wondrous had happened.

Looking back on that year, another wondrous thing had happened: I had made a friend. My very first real friend. A friend to talk to and play with. A friend to fight and dream with. A friend with whom I could morph and grow. A friend for the adventure called life.

We left Springfield for Oakland, California, in August of 1951. John David and I would connect every so often over the next decades, but it would be more than forty years before we lived near each other again. Then it would be in Washington, DC. By that time, John

David Ashcroft had served twice as attorney general of Missouri, twice as governor, one term as senator, and—during our years in DC— would become the seventy-ninth attorney general of the United States.

Relationships come and go. Some are for a season; others just for a moment. But some are for a lifetime. At this writing, John David and I have been friends for over sixty-five years!

That said, 1950 is gone forever. How people relate to each other today has been transformed. We live in a high-tech, digital world that promotes connections which often mimic relationship, but are far from what we actually yearn for when we look for meaningful community. Through our network and connections, we can have a feeling of being close without real touching. Dr. Sherry Turkle of MIT, in *Alone Together: Why We Expect More from Technology and Less from Each Other,* puts it this way:

> Technology proposes itself as the architect of our intimacies. . . . Digital connections and the sociable robot may offer the illusion of companionship without the demands of friendship. Our networked life allows us to hide from each other even as we are tethered to each other.[4]

Please understand. I love technology and social media. The ease that it offers in discovering the world is a playground for guys like me. To hear from our friends on Facebook or see our twelve grandkids' grins on Skype is wonderful. But sometimes what we *think* is happening *isn't* happening. Like an old North Carolinian friend of mine said so often, "What's happenin' ain't what's goin' on!"

The world of technology and social media can present itself in an alluring way, but it often gives me more than I want and less than I need. It changes daily. Platforms and devices shift like the weather. It offers me a lot of things and takes me lots of places. Specifically, it takes me *wide*. Where it cannot easily take me is *deep*. So, where do I go to find deep?

There is built into each of us the need not just to connect but the need to engage. As we will see, we discover ourselves as we discover each other. We adapt to change, but we yearn for stability. We love to have wings, but we also need roots. *Friendship can deliver both wings and roots.*

You already know I'm an older guy. I like to think I won't be officially old until I'm ninety. But, at this writing, I *am* on my seventy-fifth trip around the sun. So life has worked me over a bit. In the process, I've discovered that certain things make us human and certain things make life work. Old Archimedes, the greatest scientist of his day, spoke to that idea. Born in 287 BC, he described how levers work and gave us one of the most quotable lines in history: "Give me a place to stand, and I'll move the earth." It's a physics principle and a great metaphor.

Where *can* you stand to get a solid footing in life? Where *can* you really be grounded?

Ruth and I have a bias: *get relationships right and everything else follows.* Our first seven years of life were spent in very different spaces geographically, but they had a common theme: relationship was king.

We were both born in California. I was an Oakland guy, and she was a San Joaquin Valley girl. I was city. She was farm. Then things changed. At the age of three, I left all extended family and sailed to India with my parents and sister. Ruth stayed in ranch and farming country north of Modesto surrounded by grandparents, aunts, uncles, and cousins. They were her best friends.

She could run two hundred yards through a peach orchard and up the back stairs straight into her grandmother's kitchen. It was there with her grandma that she would discover canning and baking with all its delights. It was in that farmhouse that the smell of fresh-baked peach cobbler was tied to the love of her grandma—one of the deepest bonds Ruth has ever had. And it's with her still!

I, on the other hand, was running the decks of the MS *Gripsholm* (Swedish liner converted to troop ship) all across the North Atlantic from Jersey City to Alexandria, Egypt. Then, on to Bombay, India, on the RMS *Samaria* (British liner converted to troop ship) with more of the same. Churning through the chop and swells of the seas, we befriended fascinating people from around the world every day on the fantail or promenade deck or over lunch in the dining room. To this day, when I breathe in salt air, I am there again, a three-year-old finding new friends at every turn. That joy has never left!

With those scenes as a backdrop, we write this book with one thought in mind: *let's make sure of relationships.* The siren song of the immediate is all around us. Fear of Missing Out (FOMO) is so real that *distracted* and *overwhelmed* can easily define our lives. And that intimate cyber world—alive in your pocket, on your wrist, or embedded in your glasses—delivers big time. We get that. But to paraphrase Shakespeare, "*Wide* is easy, like the wind; *deep* is hard to find." Deep doesn't just happen. It happens when you get sugar on a kitchen floor and flour on your blouse front and Grandma chuckles. It happens when you explore a ship from funnel to anchor chain and your dad makes sure you don't get lost. It happens when you become the greatest tadpole hunters of all time!

The ancient prose of Ecclesiastes 4:9–12 says it best:

Two are better than one,
>because they have a good return for their work:
If one falls down,
>his friend can help him up.
But pity the man who falls
>and has no one to help him up!
Also, if two lie down together, they will keep warm.
>But how can one keep warm alone?
Though one may be overpowered,
>two can defend themselves.
A cord of three strands is not quickly broken.

These words speak to the effectiveness of our lives. When two or three walk together, it's the best.

In that spirit, as you hike trails or take road trips, gather in twos and threes for serious talk or a screaming football afternoon, have a hot beverage while munching on a Cinnabon or gluten-free something, maybe, just maybe, a few of those relationships will get tagged with that wonderful word, *friend*.

To make a friend and be called a friend is a worthy goal.

The Greek philosopher Aristotle said it so well, "Friendship is a kind of excellence and furthermore is very necessary for living."[5]

Above all, friendship does not depend on sameness. It is way more than hanging out with folks of common origin or religion or personality. After all, if sameness of personality were a litmus test, Ruth and I shouldn't work. Friendship—true, deep friendship—is found in a desire to know and the willingness to be known. It is choosing to walk with another person through whatever comes. A lasting friend knows you and still likes you. And a lasting friend, at the end of the day, is quite simply *there*.

When all is said and done, Ruth may be peach cobbler and I may be salt air, but we know what it's like to be known.

And we've been friends for more than fifty years.

That's what really matters.

RUTH'S THOUGHTS

Half a century! That's a long time to be friends. Especially when you're as different as peaches and salt air! Let me explain:

Dick is a man of many words. Most of them spoken. He believes that people want to know what he is thinking, so he talks. If no one was present to listen, he could probably talk to a wall. I am a woman of few words. Before I speak, I must mull things over and decide if anything I'm thinking is worth saying. Often I decide that it isn't.

Dick is very curious about others and life in general, and he uses most of his words to engage people. People on trains or in airplanes. People at the bank or in grocery stores. Many times he engages with people he has never met before. He sees them as friends-in-the-making. He thinks he can never have too many friends. So he has a gazillion friends. That's why he's writing a book about friendship.

Why am I helping him? I'm trying to figure that out. It's certainly not because it's easy for me to make friends. I'm more of an introvert, and to be honest, it's never been my goal to have a lot of friends. Just a few good ones—and most of them family. Until the age of seven, I grew up surrounded by family—my mother's parents and their eight children and many grandchildren. Until that age, I didn't need any other friends; these were the most important people in my life. When a move to another state necessitated making new friends, I chose three others: Ruby, Ruth, and Regina. We were the 4 Rs. In high school Mary Anne and Liz were my best friends.

Then I met Dick. At times I have been quite jealous of his uncanny ability to make a stranger a friend. He comes alive and gains energy by being with people—a lot of people! He would be very lonely going through life with just a couple of good friends. Being with lots of people drains me, and I need a good dose of solitude afterward. Put me in a room with strangers and it can turn into the loneliest place on earth. Small talk doesn't come easy for me. I am much more comfortable having tea and a chat with a couple of friends or being introduced to folks I don't know by sharing personal stories around the dinner table.

I certainly can't say, like Dick, that I've never met a stranger, but I am grateful for the wonderful friends we share—and often those friendships began as a result of Dick's engaging personality. It's taken us many years to come to a place where we feel comfortable and happy doing what we do best. I take care of the everyday details of our household and bake apple pies, while he travels the world and adds some spice and adventure. We value our friendship. It has become a safe place where we can be ourselves and welcome the differences that push us to grow.

Whether you are someone like Dick, who loves to be surrounded by friends, or like me, who is content with a trusted few, your uniqueness will help you build some great friendships if you are willing to accept others as they are. People you meet who are quite different in personality can lend balance to your perspectives and open up a whole new world to you.

Making a friend takes time and effort and perseverance. As an introvert, sometimes I've felt that it might be easier to go it alone, rather than invest in another friendship. These are my true feelings, especially when a location change has necessitated leaving behind some good friends, and making new ones seems daunting. But that's when I must stop and remind myself how lonely life would be without good friends—people who are there for me in all kinds of circumstances.

So why is this introvert helping her very outgoing, extroverted husband write this book? I'll answer that question now. I'm writing because I think there may be quite a few of you who are like me. And I think we introverts have something to say about building a few strong, lasting relationships. We may not have dozens of friends, but we're happy with the friendships we do have. I am writing to say that there is a place for us too—even if we don't use a lot of words.

FIRST THINGS

Recognize What's
True About Life

1

The Great Alone

The most terrible poverty is loneliness, and the
feeling of being unloved.

—Mother Teresa of Calcutta

On January 26, 2014, at New York City's Presbyterian Hospital,
Pete Seeger lay dying.

The ninety-four-year-old iconic singer and composer of "If I Had
a Hammer" and "Where Have All the Flowers Gone?" had been the
face of folk music and social commentary since the day he dropped out
of Harvard in 1938 to ride his bicycle across the country.

When the phone rang, it was Arlo Guthrie, son of his old friend
Woody. Pete and Arlo had played many concerts together all over the
country. After the call, he posted this to Facebook: "I simply wanted
him to know that I loved him dearly, like a father in some ways, a mentor in others and just as a dear friend a lot of the time."[1]

At 3 a.m. on January 27, Pete breathed his last. He died a man
known and loved. Who wouldn't want that? No rational person would
choose to die alone or unloved. Nothing could be emptier than that.

Between us, Ruth and I have lived in California, Oregon, India,
Missouri, Illinois, Washington, DC, and now Colorado. We have met

thousands of people and invested thousands of dollars in homes, cars, causes, travel, children, grandchildren, food, and a myriad of other things. We have discovered something in our nearly one hundred fifty combined trips around the sun: *apart from the great ideas that move us, life revolves around two things—relationships and money.* And only one of those makes us rich.

When we say, "Boy, she had a rich life!" we are not talking properties or portfolios. Those things can evaporate overnight. What creates real wealth is *friendship.* A rich life shows up in a phone call to a dying man letting him know one more time how much he is cared for.

The question is, How do we begin to build that kind of friendship? You'd think it would begin with knowing what we want. But sometimes we move forward by knowing what we *don't* want.

When my parents divorced in the early 1960s, I had a choice to make. I could submit to my fear, which entertained the idea that the patterns leading to the collapse of their marriage were genetic. Which meant that I must expect what happened to them to happen to me. Or, I could do something else. I could say to myself, "Whatever I need to do *not* to end up there, that's what I want!" I think we respond to many traumas that way. Disoriented, our emotions shattered, we say, "Whatever we need to do *never* to let *that* happen again, let's do *that.*" We frame a positive action from a negative experience. We say "No!" to the thing that steals life and "Yes!" to the thing that gives it.

FROM NEGATIVE TO POSITIVE

Is God doing that very thing when he uses *not* in the first pages of the Torah? The grand sweep of design, covenant, and truth are all there and worthy studies in themselves. The Genesis creation account is punctuated six times with the phrase "it was good." The last verse of chapter 1 even says, "God saw all that he had made, and it was *very* good."

But eighteen verses later in chapter 2, the subject of relationship is brought into focus with this sentence: "It is *not good* for the man to be alone." Adam has been created from the dust of the earth and the breath of life (see 2:7). He looks good and whole. But Yahweh says, in effect, "We're not done yet." So Eve is created. Together, they reflect who God is.

Here's the deal: it is clear that relationship existed before Adam and Eve. God was always about relationship. When he says, "Let *us* make man in *our* image," he is talking about relationship, which is in the very DNA of the Creator. So, when we hear "It is *not* good for the man to be alone," our gut says, "Aha! That's true!"

But, why tell us what we are *not* created for? Because it's simply impossible to misunderstand those ten words—"It is *not* good for the man to be alone." From childhood to old age, we all know what alone feels like.

In February of 2015, I interviewed three friends at a breakfast for business leaders in Charlottesville, Virginia. In that room of two hundred bright minds and lots of success, we explored roots and vision and faith. About two-thirds of the way into the interview, I asked the three—John Ashcroft (former Attorney General of the United States), Vern Clark (former Chief of Naval Operations), and Curt Richardson (cofounder of Otter Products)—this question: "At what moment in your life and career did you feel the most alone?" The room went absolutely still. Dead silent. Slowly their responses came. One had twice endured undeclared bankruptcy. One had to fire a subordinate, effectively ending the young man's career. One had suffered through a family tragedy. As each man answered, you could hear murmured assent. Everyone knew alone.

To be clear, alone is not the same as solitude. Alone just happens. Solitude is a choice. Theologian Paul Tillich articulated this distinction beautifully when he said, "Language . . . has created the word 'loneliness' to express the pain of being alone. And it has created the word 'solitude' to express the glory of being alone."[2] One is toxic, while the other is life giving.

The alone we speak of here is the toxic kind. That alone is unpredictable. Almost anything can trigger it. Aloneness unchecked turns us in on ourselves and destroys perspective. The gathered pain is an inch-by-inch accelerating slide off an emotional cliff. It is isolating. Left unresolved, it is a cancer.

That's why isolation is used for punishment. Emotional pain is the teacher. Alone is a time-out, when I disobey as a little guy. Alone is what happens when I behave badly as a teen and get suspended from school. When I break the law as an adult, I am separated from society and go to prison. If I am disruptive in prison, they put me where? *Solitary confinement.*

Who chooses to be alone and disoriented in the dark? No one. Who really wants to experience moments of unbridled joy or great hardship by themselves? No one. *Human contact is life itself.*

Flying home to California from the East Coast in the spring of 1992, I watched the young man sitting next to me grade English papers. Turns out he taught literature at a high school near our home. He was returning from an event where his retired navy officer father had been honored. He told me that his dad, a navy flier in the Vietnam War, had been shot down and spent several years in the infamous Hanoi Hilton prison camp. Held in isolation for weeks and months on end, prisoners used a tapping code for talking through the walls. Messaging through stone saved them. Life was found in another person, in another universe only twelve inches away.

I asked the young man, "How was your father different when he came home after those years?" He looked at me and simply said, "I loved him. When he left, he was a hard-driving high-tech fighter jock." Then, pausing with a half smile, he said, "But when he came home, he was a human being."

There you have it. Human contact is the name of the game, a mirror reflecting who we are and what we might become. It gives our lives texture and depth. It gives hope to the future and perspective to the past. Face it. The need to connect with another human being is the place we all begin.

Our earliest connection is mother and child. Studies show that as early as four months into a pregnancy a baby in utero hears its mother's heartbeat and is so comfortable in that watery womb world. Then comes the moment of delivery and the scary, intense journey out the birth canal to that bright-lighted new world populated by giants! A wise OB-GYN nurse places the newborn on the mother's stomach or at her breast. In that moment, a traumatized infant with ear pressed against the mom's chest hears the familiar beat once again. And all is well.

Scientists use the phrase *attachment theory* to describe the needed bond between a parent and child, while the phrase *attachment disorder* describes what happens when that connection is disrupted. John

Bowlby, a British psychoanalyst, first came up with attachment theory. He was trying to understand the intense distress observed in infants who had been separated from their parents. Bowlby observed that separated infants would go to extraordinary lengths (for example, crying, clinging, frantically searching) to prevent separation from their parents or to reconnect to a missing parent.[3]

Might it be that all of us, because we are fallen, experience some kind of attachment disorder? Wasn't that the consequence of being sent away from Eden? I find myself in one place when I belong in another?

We all remember places when aloneness has grabbed us. October 17, 1989, at 5:04 p.m. is time-stamped in my psyche. Driving over Highway 17 in the Santa Cruz Mountains toward Oakland, California, where I was to speak at a fund-raiser, the world exploded. Eleven miles down in the earth's crust, tectonic plates under gigantic pressure shifted three feet.

That 6.9 Richter-scale moment, later named the Loma Prieta earthquake, destroyed much of downtown Santa Cruz, flattened freeways in Oakland, set parts of San Francisco ablaze, and collapsed a section of the San Francisco–Oakland Bay Bridge. With the road cracking, huge trees whipsawing, and landslides covering roads, I somehow made it off the mountain to the town of Los Gatos. Hundreds of people milled in the streets. Bricks and glass littered sidewalks like confetti.

One thought and one thought only overwhelmed me: *I must get back to those I love.* Finding a pay phone, I dialed home. The aftershocks made the pavement shake under my feet, as sirens wailed and people shouted. And, the Great Alone had me by the throat. When Ruth said "Hello," tears came.

You've been there haven't you? When a phone call didn't just change your day—it changed your world. When what you had feared for months really did come upon you. When some failure of yours caused people to stop talking or turn away when you entered the room? And the ground shakes.

No one is impervious to feeling alone. Any trauma at any age can disorient us. When it does, the Great Alone waits in the wings. And this is not a religious or moral phenomenon; the dilemma is not a function of ethics or art or politics or age. It happens because we are human. American author John Steinbeck reflected: "We are lonesome animals. We spend all our life trying to be less lonesome."

Leanne Payne put that reflection in context when she wrote,

We are lonely, then, because we are separate. . . . Born lonely, we try hard to fit in, to *be* the kind of person that will cause others to like us. Craving and needing very much the affirmation of others, we compromise, put on any face, or many faces; we do even those things we do not like to do in order to fit in. We are bent . . . toward the creature, attempting to find our identity in him. . . . fallen man is trapped in the continual attempt to find his identity in the created rather than the Uncreated.[4]

When fractured relationships are the expected and alone becomes the order of the day, the distance and separation we feel is like leaving Eden all over again. As Adam and Eve walked out of the garden, the Great Alone was waiting.

Okay, that happened. We get it.

But that's *not* how it needs to stay. And that's *not* where we are meant to stay.

RUTH'S THOUGHTS

You sit as one apart—
  so self-possessed, so sure, so unafraid.
I quickly judge you by mind's eye
  and say, "So unlike me."
Hugging my fears, I sigh
  "No chance we could be friends."
But when you turn and look at me,
  it's in your lonely gaze I see
  that we are family.

2

The Grand Design

If you want to go quickly, go alone. If you want
to go far, go together.

—African Proverb

Something terrible has happened in New York City!"
Those chilling words ended my Tuesday breakfast with a group of
government and business friends in a stately old residence above the
Potomac River.

We got to a TV just as United Airlines Flight 175 out of Boston's
Logan Airport exploded through the South Tower of the World Trade
Center. Within the hour, the crashes in Washington, DC and Shanks-
ville, Pennsylvania, became terrible exclamation points to the original
news conveyed in one terse sentence: "The United States is under attack." It was September 11, 2001.

The combined death toll from New York City, the Pentagon, and
the Pennsylvania countryside would number 2,977 men, women, and
children from more than ninety nations. Hundreds of people known
to be in the Twin Towers were never found. Vaporized. Gone.

Precious few images bring instant emotion like the sight of smoke and flame billowing from scores of scorched windows into that blue September sky. As I write, that video runs in my head. It is unbelievable still.

Standing in that elegant Virginia home, the terror engulfed us. No one was able to stop it. This was no movie. It was real. Hour by hour, and for months afterward from the mouths of survivors, we would hear what played out on the top floors of the North and South Towers.

As the towers became furnaces that turned steel beams to liquid and spewed noxious smoke up stairwells, some—trapped by burning jet fuel—leaped from windows. It is, for me, the most haunting memory of that wretched day.

And, from the hundreds who remained, fighting for air and exit from those fiery prisons in the sky, two kinds of calls went out:

"God, help me!" and "Honey, I don't think I'm going to make it."

That day and those calls changed how I heard Jesus.

Jesus cried out like that when he himself faced death. He cried to his Father, "My God, my God, why have *you* forsaken me?"[1]

For his killers, "Father, forgive them, for they do not know what they are doing."[2]

To the repentant thief and new friend, "I tell you the truth, today you will be with me in paradise."[3]

And to his mother, Mary, and the beloved disciple, John, "'Dear woman, here is your son,' and to the disciple, 'Here is your mother.'"[4]

We know *what* he said and to *whom*. The question is, Why that reflex?

He was a rabbi/carpenter in his early thirties, who spoke with authority and healed the sick. A small-town man from the hills above Galilee, he confounded the power brokers, both religious and political. His words and actions were challenged at every turn. Disciples and critics followed him everywhere. He rankled the religious leaders simply by eating with the wrong people. It violated their sense of purity. Not only the wrong people, but at the wrong place, and never at the right time. Fast-forward to today, and the crowds he attracted would make him a YouTube sensation. Twitter would go nuts.

One day—or perhaps several because this exchange is recorded in three of the four Gospels in slightly different ways—he is asked the big question:

> "Teacher, which is the greatest commandment in the Law?"
>
> Jesus replied: "'Love the Lord your God with all your heart and with all your soul and with all your mind.' This is the first and greatest commandment. And the second is like it: 'Love your neighbor as yourself.' All the Law and the Prophets hang on these two commandments."[5]

Now, I have always understood those words as a commandment, THE commandment. But 9/11 changed that for me. On that day it became crystal clear: We are *designed* to call on God and call on each other. On that one day, I recognized that the Great Commandment is great because it fits with what I am *designed* for. I actually have the capacity to respond to it. High born or low born. Male or female. All the colors of the human family. From Cape Town to Calcutta, from Barrow to Beijing, you and I are built to reach out to God and to others. It is our deepest instinct. The Great Commandment really expresses the Grand Design.

Sometimes the cries to God and another person are so close they can almost be one and the same. They come from your built-ins—neurotransmitters in your brain that fire in nanoseconds, receptors that link you to God and the humans you love. Even if you are not convinced God really exists, in your peril you call on him. And in the next instant, you speed-dial family and friends.

The biblical notion of "loving your neighbor as yourself" when said in the same sentence with "loving God" infuses it with unique power. Does the love response in both directions come from the same place in us? Can loving my neighbor actually mean that I *am* loving God? Is this a twofer? I think it might be.

Neighbor, in practical terms, starts with the one closest to me and works its way outward—family, friends, colleagues, and so on. But Jesus pushed the boundaries. When asked "Who is my neighbor?" Jesus responded with the story of the good Samaritan (see Luke 10:29–37), which recasts the idea of neighbor by challenging the listener to be one. Jewish practice would naturally define a neighbor in technical terms to be a Jew or proselyte to Judaism, but Jesus took the Jews to a new and different place by defining *neighbor* as the one farthest out, the Gentile, the great unwashed. His approach blew the doors off their traditional understanding.

He said, "Your neighbor is the one *right there.*" You know. The one you can call. Or see. Or touch. Or the ones you meet on a jammed stairwell saturated with the smell of burning jet fuel. A stairwell soaked in fear. On 9/11, people who had never met before were bonded together for the rest of their lives. No one was debating ethics or religion. No one was questioning motive or asking about family tree.

Relationships are built three ways: through natural chemistry, over time, or under pressure. That day, as time was running out, pressure mixed with compassion and courage created a Twin Towers family. For the rest of their years, they will remember the shock and the smells, the faces and the screams, the panic and the uncertainty. Then they will remember a face and a touch and a phrase. "Come over here! Take my hand! I've got you! Let's go this way! God help us."

The need to be with others in times of crisis is so fundamental we don't even think about it. The instinct to reach for family members or close friends is reflex. It is often the difference between life and death.

On July 31, 1976, some friends of ours, with their young children, were enjoying themselves at a Colorado vacation cabin in Big Thompson Canyon. The canyon is a narrow, jagged slash in the face of the Rockies between Estes Park and Loveland with an elevation drop of about 2,800 feet in thirty miles.

About 5 p.m., a thunderstorm began dumping heavy rain high up over the headwaters of the Big Thompson River. The front didn't move. It just sat there. By 9 p.m., twelve inches of rain had fallen, and in one terrifying moment the night was shattered by a twenty-foot wall of water exploding down the canyon toward unsuspecting vacationers. That night, more than one hundred forty people died, and some bodies were never found.

Our friends Ray and Jan heard the horrific sounds and felt the earth shake. When Jan told the story, she said, "The water roared and our cabin trembled violently. The kids, terribly frightened, all piled into our bed. We held each other and prayed, thinking we were all dead. The one thought we had was, *If we are gonna go, we're gonna go together!*"

We write of these calamities to make a point, but most of our lives aren't lived under threat of imminent death. We live in the routine, the day-to-day humdrum of life. We reach out in many different ways and under many different circumstances. Our approaches to God and others are as varied as our own DNA, but our need to reach for God and reach out to others is not connected to our personality type or preferred method of communication. We can't say, "Oh, that's for verbal people—they do it so well." The reflex is visceral. It comes from a place of need that sometimes is framed in words, but always is framed in thought. And sometimes, even in action.

Consider how young children often greet a parent as Mom or Dad walks through the door after work. I like to call it a Grand Design move. And I remember it well. When I stepped through the door after a long day of work, my three-year-old daughter, Jenny, would run to me, eyes sparkling and with a winning smile. Then she made her move. Arms high over her head, she hollered: "Up, Daddy!" I dropped what I was holding and reached for her. A dad never forgets the feel of a moment like that, the spontaneous closeness. If I feel this way as an earthly father, how much more must our Heavenly Father revel in that move and that cry: "Up, Daddy!" We are designed for the move.

As we look *up* to God, it naturally leads us to look *over* at each other. But we need to get that first part right. C. S. Lewis portrayed fallen man as "bent." That is, he is looking down and, therefore, can't get life right. Leanne Payne simply said:

The *unfallen* position was, as it were, a *vertical* one, of standing erect, face turned upward to God in a listening-speaking
relationship. It was a position of receiving continually one's true
identity from God.[6]

To follow that metaphor, when we *look down,* we totally miss
what we are designed for. In writing these thoughts, I realized how
ironic it is that we live in a time in the history of mankind called the
Digital Age—an age defined by looking down. Hundreds of millions
of us, all over the world, looking down. (Says he, as he sits hunched
over his laptop typing away—looking down.) I joked just the other
day that if they dig up our bones a hundred years from now, they will
find arthritic cervical vertebrae in our necks and overdeveloped oppos-
ing thumbs!

Back to the metaphor. By definition, *designed* means "intentional,
planned." Life can corrode connectors and deplete energy, but the ar-
chitecture remains. Beneath your gifts, skills, and achievements is a
Grand Design. And it is this: You are *not* created to be *alone.* You are
created to be *together.* As you look toward God, you begin to recognize that design.

One final thought on 9/11, one of the most traumatic days in history and certainly in our lives. The events that day took me straight to
my friends. Once I knew that Ruth was safe and we were together, I
had one thought: *Where are my friends in the government who have
the responsibility to respond to this attack?*

Although we had many friends throughout the city, three of them,
John Ashcroft, Vern Clark, and Mick Kicklighter, all had huge responsibilities in their respective agencies—the US Justice Department, the

US Department of the Navy, and the US Department of Veterans Affairs. In the previous years, I had met with each of them at their offices and outside the workplace as well, just as a friend and, hopefully, an encourager. So often, I would walk away from those times, saying to myself, "How do they carry such great responsibility with such grace? I could never do that!" And, "Boy, did I learn a lot from that conversation!" Each of them was always open, always welcoming. And, we would do what friends do—laugh and eat and tell stories and pray and, on occasion, find ourselves broken before each other and the Lord. I was desperate to find them by the end of that September day.

Vern was in the Pentagon, just a few hundred feet around the corner from the point of impact. In just a few short minutes, he lost forty-two of his best and brightest colleagues. Despite the chaos, he was still able to move his team to a command center at an alternate site. He called me that evening.

As it turns out, John was midflight on his way to Milwaukee when all planes in US airspace were ordered to land at the closest airport. His Justice Department plane landed, refueled, and immediately flew back to Washington, the last miles under escort by F-16 fighters. We didn't connect till the next night.

A retired three-star Army general, Mick's role in veterans affairs was to execute the emergency plan they have in place in the event of a nuclear attack. They have huge stockpiles of medicines and access to hospitals. Mick ended up overseeing those plans from a different state. I didn't find out where he was for nine days.

In those hours and days, I reflected on the joy I had experienced with these three men over the years prior.

John and I liked nothing better than wolfing down large bowls of butter pecan ice cream, while watching ball games in his family room on Capitol Hill. When he could find time, we'd drive to his farm in the Shenandoah Valley and hike the property or pick wild blackberries. Because he loves gospel music, I'd often go and sing old songs with him that we both had learned as boys. He'd play the piano with gusto, and I'd try to sing on key!

Vern is a really fine golfer; whenever we played, he challenged me to up my game big time. We'd share great stories about his dad, who had been my mentor when I was in my twenties in Illinois. He and his wife, Connie, were the quintessential host and hostess at their residence in the Washington Navy Yard each Christmas. They were so kind to invite us to that time of wonderful food, first-class music from a brass ensemble, and all-around good cheer!

Mick and I had often met for meals at a local diner and each February we would host small groups of international leaders during the days surrounding the National Prayer Breakfast in DC. We even took a fascinating trip to India once to meet some leaders that Mick knew.

Reflecting on all those times with these men, I cannot adequately describe the relief I felt knowing my friends were safe. To physically see the guys again some days later was terrific. It was good. It was right. It was the Grand Design.

We are made for God and each other. It's a kind of coming home. We experience what Jesus dreams of when he says, "All men will know that you are my disciples, if you love one another."[7]

So, what does a God-connected friendship look like?

RUTH'S THOUGHTS

The guide instructs us carefully,
To be in groups of two or three,
But—willful, independent me,
I choose to walk alone.
So much easier, I think,
To do it on my own.

There'll be . . .
No annoying confrontations,
No obligating dependence,
No second opinions,
No risky relationships,
To slow me down.

Instead, I find . . .
No honest challenges,
No wholesome trust,
No wise alternatives,
No enriching friendships,
To grow me up.

3

What's a Friend?

When the ways of friends converge, the whole world looks like home for an hour.

—Hermann Hesse

No longer do I call you servants, for the servant does not know what his master is doing; but I have called you friends, for all that I have heard from my Father I have made known to you.

—Jesus of Nazareth, John 15:15, ESV

My favorite accolade is "My friend!" I even like it in Spanish (*"Mi amigo!"*) and French (*"Mon ami!"*). I'd probably like it in fifty-three other languages, if I knew them. It is shouted with joy across an airport terminal or whispered through tears at a graveside. It sings a song the whole world knows.

In our day, the word *friend* has been emptied of its richness. It's an overused word, much like *love*. I love pizza and the Pacific Ocean. I love a Colorado sunset and the feel of cold mountain air on my face. Oh, and I love God and my kids. What does saying, "Yeah, we're friends," mean today?

I've heard *deep friendship* defined as two people sitting together for hours in silence without feeling awkward. For a guy like me who finds it pretty tough to sit in silence for too long, that sounds incredibly hard! But beyond introversion or extroversion, the ability to sit in comfortable silence with someone is a pretty obvious example of feeling fully at home with another. There isn't a need to entertain or be entertained, just spending that time together is enough. It is a kind of quiet knowing.

So the question is, How can we get to that place with loved ones, coworkers, or neighbors?

Doesn't it make sense that, if God designs us for relationship, real friendship is fed by a growing experience of God's love? When we know down deep that we are loved, accepted, and affirmed by the God who created us and knows all about us, we are free to give ourselves to others. Ruth's notes from a talk Dr. Lloyd Ogilvie (later chaplain of the United States Senate) gave in our college chapel in the 1980s reference his words: "Don't be a stingy receiver. Let God love you. When you let God love you, you open up enough to let people love you. That's the best gift you can give them!"

Why is that idea so pivotal for human relationship? If you don't remember anything else from this book, please remember this statement:

If we are not experiencing God's love, we will always be seeking from others what only God can give. They will always fail us because we have expectations from the friendship that they cannot meet.

Henri Nouwen, the scholar, mystic, and—in his later years—caregiver, elaborates on this point:

> I discovered the real problem—expecting from a friend what only Christ can give. . . . Friendship requires closeness, affection, support, and mutual encouragement, but also distance, space to grow, freedom to be different, and solitude. To nurture both aspects of a relationship, we must experience a deeper and more lasting affirmation than any human relationship can offer. . . . When we truly love God and share in his glory, our relationships lose their compulsive character.[1]

Unrealistic expectations are killers. That's why job descriptions and performance standards are important in the business world. That's why quality premarital counseling is critical. That's why good information is key when you are getting physical therapy for that calf muscle you tore in training for a half marathon! Expectations must be managed. The question here is, What can I expect from a friendship?

That depends on what kind of friendship you are seeking. There are all different kinds of friendship—each one is inherently good. Our friends Kent and Kay Hotaling have powerfully impacted us with their thoughts on this subject:

Mentor—Mentee is a beginning place for many friendships in the body of Christ.

Short-Term—God moves us into and out of many lives, and we give ourselves to each other when we are together.

Historical—We were very important in each other's lives at
  some point in our histories, but for various reasons we
  are not a priority for each other at present.

Dormant—We are very important in each other's lives, but
  because of circumstances (for example, raising a family
  in another part of the world) in this season of life, we
  are not able to interact or be together often. But this will
  change in the next season of life.

Constant—These are the special few friends with whom we
  have the most intimacy. Two characteristics of these are
  that we mutually initiate being together, and we mutually submit our lives to each other. These are the special
  few with whom we have the greatest degree of intimacy;
  these are the friends we all long for and few have.

Their idea of constant friendship intrigues me: *"These are the
friends we all long for and few have."* Yet when people do have constant friends, it is literally life giving. A lengthy scientific study has
proven it.

Originally called the Grant Study, it now is called the Harvard
Study of Adult Development. From 1938 to 1940, a medical team selected 268 sophomore men from Harvard for a longitudinal study on
aging. It ran in tandem with the Glueck Study, which selected 456
nondelinquent young men from Boston's inner city. Amazingly, the
study has been maintained for over seventy-five years. Every two years,
interviews were conducted with participants and their spouses and
kids, blood samples taken, and even brain scans made. Sixty of the
original men are still alive at this writing.

The latest of the program's four directors, Dr. Robert Waldinger, spoke about the findings in a TED Talk he gave in Boston in December 2015. I love his title: "What Makes a Good Life? Lessons from the Longest Study on Happiness."[2] It is a picture of what we might expect of life looking ahead for eight decades.

At the outset of the study, all the men were asked, "What do you think in your lifetime would bring you happiness?" The overwhelming majority said, "Money, fame, and achievement." Recently, the same question was asked of a broad sampling of Millennials. Their answers were exactly the same.

However, what the study found after seventy-five years of monitoring the participants had very little to do with fortune, fame, or climbing the corporate ladder. The message was simple and clear, and I quote: "Good relationships keep us happier and healthier. Period!"

After seventy-five years and hundreds of thousands of dollars invested, the findings confirm what Genesis has always declared, "It is not good for the man to be alone." Who says faith and science aren't compatible?

The particulars that Dr. Waldinger presented are fascinating:

1. *Social connections are really good for us.* People who are socially connected to family, friends, and community are happier, physically healthier, and live longer.

2. *The experience of loneliness turns out to be toxic.* It kills. Lonely people are less happy, their health declines earlier in midlife, brain function declines, and they live shorter lives.

3. *The quality of close relationships makes the difference.* Bad relationships are destructive. Good relationships are protective. The predictor of long life at age fifty was not

cholesterol levels but satisfaction levels. How satisfied they
were at age fifty with their relationships predicted how
healthy they would be at eighty!

4. *Good relationships don't just protect our bodies, they
   protect our brains.* A securely attached relationship to
   another person in one's eighties has a protective effect. If
   you really feel you can count on another person in a time
   of need, your memory stays sharper longer. The relationship doesn't have to be smooth. Most good ones experience bumps in the road. It just has to answer the question
   "Can I count on you?" in the affirmative. The opposite is
   also true. When there is no one to count on, the memory
   goes.

5. *The hard work of tending to family and friends is messy,
   complicated, lifelong, never ending.*

Life is work. Without question. In life, if we work at the quality of
our relationships, they turn out to be protective and life giving. So in
our older years, when we replace workmates with playmates, we do
better. Perhaps the actual cycle of friendships goes from playmates to
classmates to workmates and back to playmates. A friend gives us
someone to count on.

Even kids know that. When I asked our fourteen-year-old grandson, Cameron, to finish the sentence "A friend is a person who . . . ,"
Cam said, "A friend is a person who sticks with you no matter what,
when you go through hard times." There you go. Someone to count
on is the doorway to happiness.

Let's hear it one more time in the researcher's words: "Good relationships keep us happier and healthier. Period!"

I love it when the Creator of the Universe and a Harvard medical team are in sync. Seriously. This is not guesswork. This is not pie-in-the-sky-bye-and-bye. This is God-spoken, research-proven truth about how people find meaning in their lives.

When Jesus said in John 10, "The thief comes only to steal and kill and destroy. I came that they may have life and have it abundantly,"[3] he really meant it. Part of his plan to give us life to the full is made clear a few chapters later, when he tells us what quality friendship is about and what a real friend looks like. A friend is someone you let in. A friend is in the know. Friends may serve you, but they are much more than servants. They lay down their lives for each other, which Jesus literally did within hours of his conversation about friendship. But he had been laying down friendship tracks for the previous three years.

Friendships matter. The light of the Grand Design chases away the darkness of the Great Alone. But how do we light that candle? How do we start the conversation? How do we lay down those tracks for friendship to run on?

It takes real honest-to-goodness conversations.

And these days conversations don't seem to come easily.

4

The Case for Conversation

Let us make a special effort to stop communicating
with each other, so we can have some conversation.

—Mark Twain

amuel Langhorne Clemens, known to most of us as Mark Twain, was a riverboat pilot, journalist, lecturer, and inventor. He was born on November 30, 1835, and died on April 21, 1910. Unsurprisingly, the America he lived in and experienced was vastly different from the America we know today. And although I have no idea in what context Twain said this, it sounds like something that could have been written yesterday. If I didn't know better, I'd think he pulled it from a blog somewhere.

And his words are so relevant, because we live in a day of communication without conversation! And we all know conversation is the basis for any relationship.

I reflect again on the exchange with the young man who said, *"I'm connected to several dozen people through Facebook and Twitter. I just don't know how to start a conversation."* I heard that statement as both a confession and a kind of plea. How do we talk to each other?

Historically, the family dinner table has been the safe place for the unending conversation. Since in many quarters that table has vanished, how do I learn to converse? Sherry Turkle distills the challenge of the lost table:

> We need family conversations because of the work they do—beginning with what they teach children about themselves and how to get along with other people. To join in conversation is to imagine another mind, to empathize, and to enjoy gesture, humor, and irony in the medium of talk. As with language, the capacity to learn these human subtleties is innate.[1]

When kids converse like that, they begin to find pleasure in being heard and understood. They begin to learn empathy, the ability to put oneself in another person's place. They start to sense the other person's feelings. They discover that family conversation is protected space and conversations can have commas in them. It is that arena in which, children can talk through feelings, rather than just act on them.[2]

Or, if the family table still exists, studies are showing that children, who quite naturally compete for their parents' attention, now have to compete with all those incoming calls and texts. In an ironic twist after twenty-plus years of digital devices, the pendulum seems to be swinging. It is the children who are beginning to ask parents to stay away from their devices during family time![3]

A DEVICE-FREE ZONE?

By the time children reach two years of age, they generally have vocabularies of two to three hundred words. That's not much, but it's plenty for communicating. There is a boatload of verbal interaction among those preschoolers. But today devices of every kind are king. It is a digital universe, and we can never go back even if we wanted to. Might the art and joy of real open-ended-take-your-chances conversation be leaking away? If so, how do we learn how to do life going forward?

Conversation is a huge factor in learning empathy. And empathy, emotional intelligence, is one of the most practical needs in today's world. When we talk to each other, we learn the worth of another's feelings, how to talk those feelings through, and how to understand and respect other people. That requires the capacity to be authentic and vulnerable, two qualities that young people today desire the most from their elders. Social media, however, teaches something completely different:

> Instead of promoting the value of authenticity, it encourages performance. Instead of teaching the rewards of vulnerability, it suggests that you put on your best face. And instead of learning how to listen, you learn what goes into an effective broadcast.[4]

We posed a question to a couple who work with young people from middle school through young professional age: "How connected does social media make us?" They thought for a few moments, then said, "It's not so much about connecting as it is about comparing and positioning." I thought, "What's wrong with that?" The world is in comparison-and-positioning mode all the time.

They explained, "Social media is not about a connection; it's about status. Kids often brag about how many Instagram friends they have. They'll make comments like, 'I don't let just *anyone* follow me.' The problem with that way of thinking is that *perceived comparison is the thief of joy.* Kids focus on whatever their lives are or where they should be or what they want and don't have. Then they put a filtered version of their life on the Internet that they can curate. The person seeing it doesn't think it's filtered. The differences are quantified by seeing what they're not included in, seeing everyone's picture-perfect life compared to their own boring ones."[5]

The Internet gives you access to a world of knowledge, and social media gives you access to a personal world of one-dimensional connections. That can really start messing with your head. Instead of adding to your life and helping you connect with those around you, it can lessen your capacity to deal with real life and to seek face-to-face interactions. Instead of helping you build a community and grow meaningful friendships, you find yourself overwhelmed with information and more isolated than before. So where do you go from there? Where can you turn when, simultaneously, you feel overwhelmed by *what* you know and you feel unsure about *who* you know?

THE VIEW FROM EDEN

Let's go back to Eden for a minute. It struck me in writing this chapter that Eden was about that very thing. God had a conversation with Adam and Eve about knowledge boundaries. But they took matters into their own hands, eating from the Tree of the Knowledge of Good and Evil. The knowledge overwhelmed them and disconnected them from God. To be clear, their core problem was their disobedience, because they had been told not to do something and then they turned right around and did it. But the net effect of their action is fascinating: *what they thought they would be getting—knowledge and control—disrupted the very thing for which they were created, authentic relationship.* They hadn't paid attention to the conversation that set the boundaries for the best relationship anyone could ever have.

So, if conversations are the fabric of relationship, how do I learn to have meaningful ones?

Celeste Headlee, a radio journalist from Georgia, gave a TED Talk titled, "10 Ways to Have a Better Conversation," which at this writing has been viewed almost four million times. She began by asking the question, "Is there any twenty-first century skill more important than being able to sustain a coherent, confident conversation?"[6] As a professional interviewer, she suggests using the ten basic rules for a good interview:

1. Don't multitask or be half in. Be present.
2. Assume you have something to learn. Don't pontificate.
3. Use open-ended questions (who, what, when, where, why, and how). Let the person describe things.
4. Go with the flow. Let stories and ideas come and go.
5. If you don't know, say you don't know.
6. Don't equate your experience with theirs.
7. Try not to repeat yourself.
8. Stay out of the weeds (people don't care about dates, et cetera).
9. Listen! Listening is the #1 most important skill. We like to talk, but our brains only allow us to talk at 225 words per minute. We can listen at 500 words per minute.
10. Finally, be brief and prepare to be amazed!

When I listened to her thoughts, I was struck by the practicality of them. Anyone can converse that way, and these practices are totally doable—even for those of us who struggle with striking up and maintaining good conversations. Even if you landed on just five of the ten things, it would make a huge difference in how you engaged with others.

THE ONE-ANOTHER EXPERIENCE

The give-and-take of conversation makes for mutuality. Scripture describes such mutual engagement with two words: *one another.* Jesus, of course, championed that practice to his followers when he told them where two or three agreed together in his name, he would be present. It is a practice encouraged again and again in the New Testament, fifty-nine times to be precise. Here's what it sounds like:

- Love each another. (John 15:17)
- Be devoted to one another in brotherly love. (Romans 12:10)
- Honor one another above yourselves. (Romans 12:10)
- Live in harmony with one another. (Romans 12:16)
- Stop passing judgment on one another. (Romans 14:13)
- Accept one another, then, just as Christ accepted you. (Romans 15:7)
- Instruct one another. (Romans 15:14)
- Speak to one another with psalms, hymns and spiritual songs. (Ephesians 5:19)
- Submit to one another out of reverence for Christ. (Ephesians 5:21)

All these experiences are rooted in conversation.

All of them take a sincere interest in the other person.

All of them require listening and responding.

All of them need authenticity and vulnerability.

From our earliest days, we work at communicating with those closest to us. Some wit in years past even observed, "Babies speak several languages before they find one their parents can understand!" But those babies soon acquire the skill for conversation and are off to the races. The capacity to think clearly and share ideas is foundational for all that follows.

Flying in to San Jose, California, from the East Coast a few years ago, my seatmates were CEOs from two computer firms in Boston. Since I was working as a college administrator at the time, I asked, "What majors do you hire out of college? Business administration or computer science?"

They said, "Hardly any business administration and only some in computer science. Mostly we hire English majors."

"Wow! Really?" I said. "Why?"

"Because English majors have been taught to think critically and are able to speak and write their thoughts in a succinct manner. Our industry is built around teams and conversing clearly is very important to us. We can always teach them the technical stuff!"

When real conversation happens, it doesn't get far before anecdotes and stories start being told. And when conversations turn to storytelling, the real person begins to stand up. God knows that's true. That's how he made us. The Creator who speaks the universe into being is the best Talker of all.

And he is the best Storyteller by a country mile.

STORYTELLERS

Story Is the Soil from Which Friendship Grows

5

God, the Storyteller

Jesus was not a theologian. He was God who
told stories.

—Madeleine L'Engle, *Walking on Water:*
Reflections on Faith and Art

Story is the big thing in relationships. We don't just have stories—we are stories. And story is rooted in God himself.

Genesis tees up the Big Story with "In the beginning." It promises
the long view. It's the original "Once upon a time" story of love gone
wrong and love redeemed. This is the Indianapolis 500 announcer
saying "Drivers! Start your engines!" We can't wait to see what happens next. There's a villain and a hero, and you and I make an appear-
ance too. And nobody does story like God.

The culture of the West has been shaped by ancient stories from
the East. They are the earliest images of life: Adam and Eve in the
Garden of Eden, David and Goliath, Jonah and the big fish, Mary and
Joseph and the birth of Jesus, Jesus walking on water. The themes are
good versus evil, the power of both good and bad choices, winning
against great odds, and sometimes the need for miracles.

All those pieces make up the Grand Story. It's a template for our own. So when one of my professors would intone, "Don't get your theology from the narrative," it made me a bit crazy. I've discovered that there is abundant, solid theology in the narrative. Truths come alive as you tramp through the wilds and barrens of life. It's through the stories that you come to understand the joy, anger, frustration, greed, generosity, and sorrow of the players. It is there that love and lust, history and dreams, the human and the divine battle it out. *Story wraps flesh around truth.*

We see it most in the life of Jesus. The hours before Jesus died are crammed with the core things that he wanted his followers to know. He poured out his heart to them. John's gospel captures his words:

> My command is this: Love each other as I have loved you. Greater love has no one than this, that he lay down his life for his friends. You are my friends if you do what I command. I no longer call you servants, because a servant does not know his master's business. Instead, I have called you friends, for everything that I learned from my Father I have made known to you.[1]

He spent three years with them, and they watched him perform miracle after miracle. They saw him tender, they saw him angry, and they heard his stories again and again. The secret of his Father's heart is revealed in those stories, none more clearly than the tale of the lost son. Immortalized in oils by the Rembrandts of the world, it may be the best short story ever told:

Jesus continued: "There was a man who had two sons. The younger one said to his father, 'Father, give me my share of the estate.' So he divided his property between them.

"Not long after that, the younger son got together all he had, set off for a distant country and there squandered his wealth in wild living. After he had spent everything, there was a severe famine in that whole country, and he began to be in need. So he went and hired himself out to a citizen of that country, who sent him to his fields to feed pigs. He longed to fill his stomach with the pods that the pigs were eating, but no one gave him anything.

"When he came to his senses, he said, 'How many of my father's hired men have food to spare, and here I am starving to death! I will set out and go back to my father and say to him: Father, I have sinned against heaven and against you. I am no longer worthy to be called your son; make me like one of your hired men.' So he got up and went to his father.

"But while he was still a long way off, his father saw him and was filled with compassion for him; he ran to his son, threw his arms around him and kissed him.

"The son said to him, 'Father, I have sinned against heaven and against you. I am no longer worthy to be called your son.'

"But the father said to his servants, 'Quick! Bring the best robe and put it on him. Put a ring on his finger and sandals on his feet. Bring the fattened calf and kill it. Let's have a feast and celebrate. For this son of mine was dead and is alive again; he was lost and is found.' So they began to celebrate.

"Meanwhile, the older son was in the field. When he came near the house, he heard music and dancing. So he called one of the servants and asked him what was going on. 'Your brother has come,' he replied, 'and your father has killed the fattened calf because he has him back safe and sound.'

"The older brother became angry and refused to go in. So his father went out and pleaded with him. But he answered his father, 'Look! All these years I've been slaving for you and never disobeyed your orders. Yet you never gave me even a young goat so I could celebrate with my friends. But when this son of yours who has squandered your property with prostitutes comes home, you kill the fattened calf for him!'

"'My son,' the father said, 'you are always with me, and everything I have is yours. But we had to celebrate and be glad, because this brother of yours was dead and is alive again; he was lost and is found.'"[2]

Now *that's* a story! My Western mind gets the overall gist of it, but Middle Eastern listeners would have been stunned. Living in a world of traditions and tribal thinking, rooted in centuries of practice, Jesus paints a picture that blows out tradition. He wants us to *feel* how God responds to things like greed and betrayal and lack of honor. He wants us to *see* people the way that God, the Father, sees them. He tells us a story so flagrant and so opposite to my understanding of honor in a tribal culture that it's almost impossible to listen to, let alone hear it!

When I read this story—two thousand years later in a Western setting, even I can feel the emotion. As a father and grandfather, I am on the edge of my seat. This is father-and-son stuff:

It had been forever.

How many days had the old man scanned the hills looking for his wandering son? How many nights had he prayed to Yahweh to keep him safe? How many servants had he sent to distant places seeking word of his boy?

And suddenly there he was!

The Jewish lad who had profaned his faith and spit on the family name comes to himself slopping hogs in a foreign country. The only safe place he knows is his father's house, so he heads for home.

Dignity left at the door, the father begins to walk toward the distant figure. He walks faster. He begins a hobbling run, shouting, "My son, my son, you're home at last!" Effusive joy explodes from long nights of longing, prayer, and hope. The self-pitying, easily offended, or embarrassed person would long ago have given up. But not this tenacious father, one who loved his son no matter what.

And now the old man has his boy back. Neither his old age nor his son's stupidity would deny him. The account says, "That while he was still a long way off his father saw him and was filled with compassion for him; he ran to his son, threw his arms around him and kissed him." This was no rush to judgment. This was a rush to celebrate.

What a picture! It captures the love and lust and pettiness and intrigue that brackets so much of life. The pain shows up in real people with real flaws. But to Middle Eastern ears, nothing about this tale makes any sense. It's about a younger son who, by asking for his inheritance, says to his father, "I wish you were dead!" He takes off to squander his dad's hard-earned monies in wild living. He is, literally, throwing away his father's life like there is no tomorrow.[3] The word *prodigious* is defined as "extensively great in size, extent, or degree."[4] That's where we get the traditional title for this story, the Prodigal Son. The self-centered boy is a spender. And he ends up in the worst place a Jewish kid could end up: *feeding pigs in a foreign land. He's down in the mud with a Gentile's hogs.*

According to tradition, he deserves to die in his hometown, the ancestral village. More to the point, he should die at the hand of his father. He has humiliated not just his father and the family, but the entire community. It doesn't get worse than that.

But in this story, the old man hikes up his robe and *runs* to the boy. No elder does *that*. It isn't done. It's not right. The perpetrator is supposed to come and grovel. But the father will have none of it.

In my mind's eye, the boy's willingness to grovel is silenced by a father's finger on the boy's lips. "But I'm not worthy" is muted by the father's voice. "That's my call, not yours. You had your day and your say—this is mine. Servants, bring the robe, the shoes, and the ring. You wish me to make a judgment? There it is. Take it or leave it, but you will not change it!" What's wrong is made right. The lost has been found. The dead has been raised to life.

At the moment of truth, the listeners are in shock. They get the opposite of what they expect. Instead of a killing, they get a killer party. Mercy wins the day!

What's that about? It's about the entrance of a new kingdom. It is antithetical to all they have known for generations. It makes no sense. The new kingdom introduces a new King, with new rules and new outcomes.

I have read the narrative scores of times over the years and have asked myself the question, "Who are you in this story?" In a story like this, it's almost natural to try to place ourselves in the place of the prodigal or even see ourselves in the scornful eyes of the elder brother. But in the story of the Gracious Father, the real kicker to the story isn't where we fit. Instead, it's what our Father sees when looking at us. Through the words of this parable, we hear everything we need to know about who he is and who he believes us to be. When he tells that story, we absolutely see the heart of the Father. And if we respond, we can never get over it.

Nobody told a better story than Jesus of Nazareth. It's true that he walked in a culture of rabbis and peripatetic teachers who taught by parable and anecdote. But according to his listeners, his stories rang with disturbing originality and authority. He defined what it means to be original. At the heart of it all, he is connecting with us by revealing himself. Along the way, I get to decide if I believe him. Like Frederick Buechner says:

> It is to choose to believe that the truth of our story is contained in Jesus's story, which is a love story. Jesus's story is the truth about who we are and who the God is who Jesus says loves us.

It is the truth about where we are going and how we are going
to get there, if we get there at all, and what we are going to find
if we finally do.[5]

The late Southern storyteller and novelist Pat Conroy once said,
"And a great story changes the world for you—changes the way you
look at life."[6]

Why do you think that might be? I think it's because God put the
love of story at the heart of humankind. He gave us a way to share our
lives and memories that depends on nothing but the willingness to
speak and listen. It is not Greek rhetoric. It is not a classroom lecture.
It is a thing of history and imagination. God telling his story says,
"Come know me."

Story is built into the fabric of humanity.

6

Man, the Storyteller

The story—from *Rumpelstiltskin* to *War and Peace*—is one of the basic tools invented by the mind of man for the purpose of understanding. There have been great societies that did not use the wheel, but there have been no societies that did not tell stories.

—Ursula K. Le Guin

Tell me a story!" echoes in every culture on earth.

Story inspires civilizations, passes truth from generation to generation, and connects us to each other. It has been the great teacher through all of human history. Stories are powerful because they have mystery and beauty, laughter and tears, anger and poignancy that draw us to them. They are heard everywhere, over campfires and around kitchen tables, in cars and on planes. And always, always at family gatherings.

Why the big emphasis on story, you ask? Simple. Storytelling provides a pathway to knowledge and friendship. It is how we humans share our lives with others. Studies show that children by the age of two begin to create and tell their own stories. In the telling, they explain their worlds and learn about the worlds of others. In some cases, that's how they learn to manage their worlds. It is intuitive and natural. *We are built for it.*

Tales told by the old to the young have passed down family lore through the centuries. According to Jeremy Hsu in *Scientific American,* storytelling is a human universal, and common themes appear in tales throughout history and all over the world. "The best stories—those retold through generations and translated into other languages—do more than simply present a believable picture. These tales captivate their audience, whose emotions can be inextricably tied to those of the story's characters."[1]

No one in the last hundred years, in my view, did that better than Alex Haley in his seminal work, *Roots.* It swept us away as a TV miniseries in 1977, and a remake aired on the History channel in the spring of 2016. A career US Coast Guardsman, Haley had been fascinated as a child by his family history told on the front porch of his grandmother's Tennessee home. When he would visit in the summers, she told of the "Furthest-Back person" in their family, a boy named "Kintay" who had been kidnapped as a youth and brought to Annapolis, Maryland, to be sold. He was simply called "the African."

After many years of searching, Haley located a tribe he thought might be his people near the Gambia River in Africa. He traveled to the village of Juffure, where the griot (gree-oh)—the tribal historian—lived. Haley spoke of that moment, as the two of them sat on low stools:

> The musicians had softly begun playing *kora* and *balafon,*
> and . . . the griot, aged 73. . . . began speaking the *Kinte* clan's
> ancestral oral history; it came rolling from his mouth across the

next hours . . . 17th and 18th century Kinte lineage details. . . .
It was as if some ancient scroll were printed indelibly within the
griot's brain.[2]

Then he got to the part that Haley had heard so many times before at his grandmother's feet on that old Tennessee porch:

About that time the king's soldiers came, the eldest of these
four sons, Kunta, when he had about 16 rains, went away from
his village, to chop wood to make a drum . . . and was never
seen again.[3]

Overwhelmed, Haley told the griot that Kunta was his ancestor.
The villagers began to dance, and young mothers ran up to thrust
babies into his arms for blessing. And Haley couldn't stop himself
from weeping:

Let me tell you something: I am a man. But I remember
the sob surging up from my feet, flinging up my hands and
bawling as I had not done since I was a baby. . . . If you really
knew the odyssey (a powerful story going for generations) of
us millions of black Americans, if you really knew how we
came in the seeds of our forefathers, captured, driven, beaten,
inspected, bought, branded, chained in foul ships, if you really
knew, you needed weeping.[4]

In Haley's recounting, the griot was pivotal in that moment. Gri-
ots are people gifted to carry the history of peoples in their heads and

hearts. Such storytellers have been central figures in society for thousands of years.

> Storytelling was popular because before writing was developed,
> the success of communication was measured largely by how
> much of it was remembered by the audience. They couldn't
> just go write it down. So a high value was placed on techniques
> that helped people remember things, like the rhythm of song,
> the rhyme of a poem, or the engagingness of a story.[5]

In a world without books or the Internet, the storyteller was a mobile news anchorman. He traveled from place to place bringing the latest accounts of what was going on in this town or that. Sometimes he put the stories to song and they called him a minstrel or troubadour. Clarissa Pinkola Estés, with great humor, captured it:

> Modern storytellers are the descendants of an immense and
> ancient community of holy people, troubadours, bards, griots,
> cantadores, cantors, traveling poets, bums, hags and crazy
> people.[6]

In a downloadable culture of e-books and audio books, we forget that mass-produced printed books have only been around for the last seven hundred years. The advent of Johannes Gutenberg's printing press in the mid-1400s changed the face of the world. It spread information and ideas at a phenomenal rate. The written word began to replace the spoken story. The trade-off, of course, was the loss of tone and gesture and inflection and emotion. But, spoken or written, story itself did not get lost.

Screenwriter Randall Wallace, whose credits include the screen-plays for *We Were Soldiers, Secretariat,* and the story of his ancestor, William Wallace, in *Brave Heart,* keynoted the 2011 National Prayer Breakfast in Washington, DC.

He spoke about the impact of story in recounting his life as a boy in rural Tennessee. When he was battling asthma to the point of not being able to sleep, his grandmother would hold him close all night and rock him in her old rocking chair. Sitting in the audience, I was touched when I heard him say, "She would rock and sing and tell me stories of her childhood along with stories from the Bible. At my age, I could not tell the difference."

Like creeks tumbling into rivers, stories feed our lives. And what variety! Aesop's Fables make a practical point. Fairy tales take us to other worlds. Murder mysteries challenge our brains. Romance novels recall our youthful days. And all of us learn from stories. Whether we learn best by seeing, listening, or doing, storytelling speaks to all three types of learners.[7]

And how children respond! Being in the room when children are hearing a story is a special kind of experience. Whatever the kind of tale, children want to know one thing when they hear the words *the end.* And that is, Is that story true? Because true stories are the best, aren't they?

True-to-life anecdotes reveal a real, touchable human being. The snapshots can be garden variety or extraordinary, but they freeze-frame moments in a person's life that have made them who they are.

It can be an old uncle who describes in halting detail the Battle of the Bulge in World War II, where he came close to freezing to death. Surrounded by the enemy, he never thought he would see the age of twenty. Or it can be the apostle Paul telling of his face-to-face with Jesus on the Damascus road. Blinded by the Light, he is in limbo for three days. With past certainties shaken and his future unsure, he is transformed from religious jailer to spiritual liberator. His life whipsaws one hundred eighty degrees in seventy-two hours. And because he tells the story, we are blessed—two thousand years down the road.

In later life, he wrote friends in a town called Philippi in northern Greece, offering his own snapshot of a changed life:

> If anyone else thinks he has reason for confidence in the flesh,
> I have more: circumcised on the eighth day, of the people of
> Israel, of the tribe of Benjamin, a Hebrew of Hebrews; as to
> the law, a Pharisee; as to zeal, a persecutor of the church; as
> to righteousness under the law, blameless. But whatever gain
> I had, I counted as loss for the sake of Christ.[8]

We owe the storyteller. From oral historians of great repute to the great-aunt who kept track of the family tree in her big Bible, the story gets passed on. They tell us what people's lives were like then, so we can know better who we are now.

Broadway and Hollywood have always known that to be true. No company in recent years has captured that truth better than Pixar Animation Studios, a company focused on computer-generated animation features to the delight of young and old alike, who have spent fanciful hours watching everything from *Toy Story* to *Finding Nemo* to, my favorite, *Up*.

When author Brené Brown visited Pixar some years ago, the sign on the wall of Pixar's Story Corner caught her eye:

Story is the big picture.
Story is process.
Story is research.[9]

With that template in mind, it is now our turn. Each of us has a story. That narrative is the foundation for every relationship. When I speak about my own early years, I am back in 1947 British colonial India. I am riding a coal-and-steam-driven narrow-gauge train called the Blue Mountain Express up into the tea plantations of the southern mountains to go to boarding school. The picture has rainbow colors and smells of sweat and cow dung and tea-on-the-bush. It has become one of the lenses through which I see the world.

God's story is a lens like that. It presents a totally different view of life. And, to a lesser extent, your own story lens does that. When you tell your story, it changes the way the listener sees the world: *Your* story is an original and, when *you* tell it, the door to a possible friendship swings open. Another person can walk through that door into your world. Then you walk through that person's story into theirs.

Once upon a time you were alone. Once upon a time you sensed there was more. Once upon a time you made a decision to tell and hear a story. And it changed everything.

In a world inundated by data and information, where is the narrative that transcends it all? In a world of snippets and snapshots, where are the themes that tie it all together? Stories do not just inform us. They form us. They put sinew and muscle on skeletal ideas and the bones live.

You have a story to tell. What memories do *you* pull up? What adventures do *you* retell? What times do *you* relive? What is the lens through which *you* see life?

Why should I tell my story, you ask? Because the telling and the hearing of your story brings understanding—and that is the pathway to friendship. Telling your story gives friendship a chance.

Without your story, friendship has no chance at all.

RUTH'S THOUGHTS

Did you grow up hearing stories about people you admired? Not storybook characters, but real people with true stories? If you were hearing about people in your family, the stories carried import far beyond the spoken words. In some mysterious way you became connected to someone who was part of your heritage. As you listened, you learned some of the triumphs and pitfalls of their journeys, discovered their beliefs, and identified some family traits. Really, you found out more about yourself. And you were actually learning how to piece together the material that would be the fabric of your own story.

When I sit on the little block wall of my raised vegetable garden, dig my hands into the rich soil, and tug at the weeds that grow faster than my tomatoes, I think about my granddad. The stories he told and the way he lived his life have impacted me. He was a farmer all of his years—first in his native state of Indiana, then a wheat farmer on the Canadian prairies, and finally a peach rancher in California's San Joaquin Valley. For seven years I lived just down the path from my grandparents' house in Modesto, and later I spent some summers there. That's where I really got to know them.

I loved Granddad's farming stories. He told of Indiana cornfields so vast and level in height that it looked like a giant floor stretching to the horizon. And I was fascinated when I heard about the huge challenges he faced as a homesteader in Canada—winters so cold that his moustache would freeze to the ice crystals on his face and the blade of an axe could break while chopping wood. While he spoke, his philosophy of life came through. Simply put, you did what you had to do.

Granddad's faith was just a fact. His trust in God was built on the solid experience of a lifetime. He was eager to tell his grandchildren stories of times when the odds were against him but God was for him. I came to believe that prayer was an integral part of life. It was not only something you did when life was overwhelming you, but you also expressed gratitude for his provisions at the dinner table and always at the end of your day.

Some of his prayers involved high drama, and the recollection of stories about them still inspires me. You can imagine what a move to virgin Canadian prairie might entail. My grandparents took all their household goods, four horses, a cow, two mules, Granddad's English setter hunting dog, and some farm machinery on the train.[10] The livestock was in a freight car. During the journey, there was a train collision and several cars were pushed off the track and overturned. The car with Granddad's stock remained upright and intact. He always gave God the credit for protecting that train car.

The other prayer that stuck with me had to do with Granddad's second wheat crop in Canada. While out walking in his fields that were ready for harvest, he saw an angry looking cloud in the distance that would likely bring hail. He needed the money from the sale of the wheat to pay his bills and provide for his family during the winter, so he asked God to spare his crop. The hail storm passed over his acreage without doing any damage. And he was able to provide seed wheat for the spring season to his neighbors who had lost their crops. It seemed to me, from these stories, that if you relied on God, you could handle most anything that came your way.

A close second to reliance on God was Granddad's ability to rely on himself in most situations. Life hadn't been easy for him. His father died when he was three. When his mother re-married five years later, he couldn't get along with his stepdad. At eight years of age, he made the big decision to leave their home and move in with his grandparents, who lived in the same town. When Granddad showed up, his grandparents were in their midfifties, with twelve children of their own, the youngest still at home.

In such a large household, it was inevitable that things did not always please him. His one complaint that I remember him mentioning was that he had to eat leftovers in the kitchen, after the adults had eaten. That may have been a common practice back then, but it didn't sit well with Granddad. He promised himself that when he had children and grandchildren of his own, they would be served their meals before the adults. He kept that promise. We always ate first.

Hard work was something Granddad learned at an early age. I loved the story he told about moving a herd of cows through the streets of their town when he was only nine years old. To me, it didn't matter that he lost control of the herd and, as he told it, cows went everywhere. He gave it his best and that was what mattered. As he grew, his grandfather taught him carpentry skills, and together they built a barn with a beam-and-post framework held together by wooden pegs.

A homesteader, Granddad would need all the experience he had gained during those years with his grandfather. When he and Grandma arrived in Canada in the spring of 1906, they found their claim was unbroken prairie as far as the eye could see. The Dominion Land Policy required that they build a house and clear a certain amount of land so they could plant a crop. Shelter had to be built for the farm animals, a fireguard ploughed, a vegetable garden planted, game hunted to supplement the food supply, and a clean water supply found.[11]

The demands must have seemed overwhelming, especially with the constant threat of drought, wildfires, hailstorms, and invading grasshoppers. But with God's help and hard work, they persevered, and this became their home for thirteen years. The fact than an uncle and his family had become homesteaders on the Canadian prairie before them must have helped. And the fact that they had traveled together with Grandma's sister and husband and child must have helped. They weren't doing this alone. They would be friends among friends, facing the unknown together.

Now I wish I had asked Granddad more questions and learned more about his life. I wish I'd told him how much I admired him. Perhaps you can relate when you think of those who helped shape your life. As a child, I dreamed of growing up and living on a farm just like Granddad's. Of course, I didn't realize that farming was one of the most difficult and time-consuming jobs in the world. So, thankfully, the closest I've come to living that dream is having a backyard garden that I've squeezed into nearly every place we've lived.

If you ask Dick, I believe he will agree that some of that self-sufficient spirit and the willingness to tackle difficult projects has been passed down to me. At times, I must seem persistent against all odds. You might call it stubbornness. He probably thinks that if I've made up my mind to do something, he might as well give in. And I think he's right!

Did Granddad know what he was teaching me when he shared his stories, illustrating for me how he lived his life? Did he know I was listening and watching? Did he know that his words and actions were drawing me toward his values and what he thought was important? I don't know. What I do know is that he absolutely affected how I wanted to live my life. And I'm grateful.

Your Starting Place

Indeed, our story is finally all any of us owns,
because, as I once told my grandson, a story
has only one master.

—Frank Delaney, *Ireland*

Earliest memories are the starting place for every relationship we
will ever have.

The bassoon bellow from high above the waterline was unforgettable. The MS *Gripsholm* sounded her whistle as she backed out of her berth in Jersey City harbor en route to the Mediterranean. It was September of 1945, and I was three years old. That's one of my first memories.

Each person's story has a beginning, and it's found in first memories. Just the size of the world sets it up. When we are small, all things are huge and every adult a giant. First impressions are the order of the day, as we grow up. Life is a series of firsts: a first ball game, a first day of school, a first friend, a first house, a first sibling, a first broken bone, a first airplane ride. It goes on and on. Our early years are the first chapters of our biographies.

Dr. Dan Allender, in his insightful book *To Be Told: God Invites*

You to Coauthor Your Future, explains why our personal stories are the main building blocks for friendship. He says that the telling and writing of your own story is critical to understanding your entire life:

> Most of us have spent more time studying a map to avoid getting lost on a trip than we have studying our life so we'll know how to proceed into the future.[1]

> Our story is truer than any other reality we know. . . . When I study and understand my life story, I can then join God as a coauthor.[2]

WHO AM I? AND WHERE WAS I? ARE THE SAME QUESTION

I don't know when I first grappled with the core question, Who am I? What I do know is that I've asked it lots of times since then, and I know that it's connected to another question: Where do I come from? They are two sides of the same coin. *Where I come from is a huge part of who I am.* Ask any Texan or Irishman, any Chinese businessperson or Armenian farmer. Ask an only child or someone with eight siblings. Where I come from really influences how I see myself.

Think of the stories you pay money to see. The great stories of stage and screen are centered in a *where.* From *Les Misérables* to *West Side Story,* from *Schindler's List* to *Hamilton,* the geographic roots of the lead character's life set the stage for everything that follows.

Narrative always starts with a *where.* God gives Adam and Eve a where at the start of the Grand Story. It is a garden called Eden and their job is to be horticulturalists. The only exception was a single tree in the middle of the garden. The command was simple: "Don't eat from it." They thought a tiny bite wouldn't hurt. And there you go. Knowledge dawns and the Great Alone begins to nibble at them. And then, the God who has designed them for relationship comes for a visit.

> Then the man and his wife heard the sound of the LORD God
> as he was walking in the garden in the cool of the day, and
> they hid from the LORD God among the trees of the garden.
> But the LORD God called to the man, "Where are you?"
> He answered, "I heard you in the garden, and I was afraid
> because I was naked; so I hid."[3]

Adam and Eve have crossed the line and know it. Seeing they are naked, they run for cover behind a tree, like children putting a blanket over their heads, thinking the parent cannot see. God is looking. Adam and Eve are hiding.

Really? This is God, for Pete's sake. And, with a rhetorical question, God calls Adam out. "Where are you?" The question needs reflection, not a response. He knows very well where Adam is. It's Adam who doesn't know where he is. Adam and Eve's disobedience disorients their lives and muddies their identities. It costs them the *where* that makes sense of things. Knowing your *where* is an organizing piece of your life; it is essential to your story.

The simple practice of asking the where questions about your own history is the seedbed for future friendship. Coming back to Alex Haley's story for a moment, there is a scene from the original *Roots* miniseries that sticks with me to this day. Kunta Kinte has a daughter named Kizzy who is courted by an American-born slave named Sam. Ultimately she decides not to marry him. When asked why she made that decision, her answer reflects a practical wisdom that went something like this: "Sam ain't American. He don't know Africa. He cain't understand Africa. And if you don't know where you comes from, you cain't know where you're goin'!" When I heard those words, it was a moment. It was so counterintuitive, that it felt like the Bible. Simply put, if you want to go forward you need to glance in the rearview mirror.

LOOKING BACK TO MOVE FORWARD

Let's look at the *where* of our lives. Where we come from experientially really shapes us. And part of that is the *where* of the geography and cultures we come from. Ruth and I come from neighboring-but-different ethnic roots. She is French, English, German, and Scots-Irish. I am German and Scots-Irish. Her people came to Virginia and North Carolina and ended up in California. My people came to Michigan and Kansas and ended up in California. It is in those facts that she and I find our place.

Ruth and I took a trip to the British Isles in 1992 to check out our roots. To be clear, "checking out roots" is often what people do when they've traveled a bunch of times around the sun and have more years behind them than ahead of them. Though we may not always recognize it, I believe we intuitively want to know our historical *where* no matter what our age. On that trip, we discovered a delightful thing!

The challenge in our search had been where to start on the ground. Our ancestors left their countries of origin in the 1700s and 1800s. To their families and friends, they might as well have fallen off the face of the earth because they were illiterate and couldn't write home. So, two centuries later, Ruth and I were there on the hunt for connections. Google and Ancestry.com didn't exist back then, so we had gone to the Sutro Library in San Francisco and the National Archives in Washington, DC, to research the country of Ruth's family origins. Scotland it was.

With that information in hand, we headed out to see if we could find the people from our past. How do you do that in a practical way? We had a crazy idea. It was a thought that no self-respecting young person would ever think of, we've been told. With a local phone book in hand, we decided to look up someone with Ruth's family name. Then we cold-called that number to see what would happen.

The delightful thing we discovered was this: *the family name worked like magic.* We could pick any Blakeley out of the book and, upon calling, be invited to lunch or tea. What fun. We could literally eat our way across Scotland!

In a village just north of Ayr on Scotland's southwest coast I found one of those cool and quaint phone booths on a downtown corner. We had a system: Ruth found the name in the phone book and I made the call. I was calling a Blakeley whom we had been told might have some information. When he answered, I said that we were exploring our roots and asked if he could help.

"Where did your people settle?" he asked in a lovely Scottish burr.

"North of Knoxville, Tennessee," I said.

"Och, my people went to Pennsylvania," he said.

"What did they do?" he asked.

"I think they were weavers," I replied.

"Och, my people were miners."

"Can you tell me anything more about them?" he said.

"Well," I said, "the records show that in 1801 two of the Blakeley men got thrown out of Paw Paw Baptist Church on the banks of the Holston River for drinking and fighting."

Whereupon, Mr. Blakeley exclaimed, "Aha! I think we may be related!"

GEOGRAPHY AND FRIENDSHIP

Places connect and define us. *Geography* is "the study of the physical features of the earth and its atmosphere, and of human activity as it affects and is affected by these, including the distribution of populations and resources, land use, and industries."[4] Oh, to have been an explorer back in the day! What must it have been like to make a pencil sketch of a coastline from the quarterdeck of a Spanish frigate in the 1600s? Or sail through what then were called the Sandwich Islands and we know today as Hawaii? Growing up I used to say, "Give me the *National Geographic* and the Bible and I'm good." Those two works opened up the whole universe to my young dreaming mind, because I found where I was and who I was in both places.

A friend of ours says that the Grand Story is about places and people. Places tell the story of people from the Garden of Eden to the Heavenly City. And the place names really do focus the story, don't they? The tale is told by recounting what happened at the Red Sea and Mount Sinai, Bethlehem and Golgotha, Jerusalem and the Damascus Road.

Not long after arriving in Washington, DC, I was thinking through how to tell the story of Jesus in this place where power and poverty live side by side. It is one of the few cities in the world designed to be the capital of a country. It really is three overlapping cities. The District is comprised of the folks who live and work within its limits and for whom it is home. Then, there's the federal capital, which most of us think of when we say, "Washington, DC." Finally, there's the international community living in the embassies of more than 175 nations, many of which are clustered along the length of Massachusetts Avenue Northwest.

So, how do you tell the Jesus story across all those lines of ethnicity, politics, and religion? It came to me as a study in *where*. I can't point to a moment, but over some days this imaginary conversation got framed in my head:

Jesus says, "Foth, here's the plan.

I'll leave my *place*.

I'll come to your *place*.

I'll take your *place*.

Then we'll go to my *place!*"[5]

Whether your place happens to be an elegant residence on Embassy Row in DC or a roach-infested urban project building, it makes not one wit of difference to him. Regardless of where you find yourself, God will go there to meet you—every time.

If the Grand Story is all about heaven come to earth and the Creator of the Universe showing up in a cradle, we should not be surprised then that a friendship might begin with a geographic question: "So where are you from originally?"

8

How to Read a Walking Book

Then Shaphan the secretary informed the
king, "Hilkiah the priest has given me a
book." And Shaphan read from it in the
presence of the king.

—2 Kings 22:10

What do you do if you become a king at the age of eight?

You do the best you can. And by all indications, King Josiah of Judah was the best. He ruled for thirty-one years, and he changed the face of the nation—for the better. Unlike his father, Amon, and grandfather, Manasseh, Josiah, as a young man, chose to follow the Lord. We aren't told in the record how he knew about the Lord. I'd like to believe it was through stories handed down from father to son. Whatever the case, the teenage king made his move:

In the eighth year of his reign, while he was yet a boy, he began to seek the God of David his father, and in the twelfth year he began to purge Judah and Jerusalem of the high places, the Asherim, and the carved and the metal images.[1]

The house of the Lord had crumbled over the decades and Josiah ordered its restoration. As the builders started the work, they found a book, which they gave to Josiah's aide. The aide, excited I'm sure, went to the young king and said, "Hilkiah the priest has given me a book." Not any old book. This was The Book, the scrolls of the Law of Moses, unread for years. When Shaphan read The Book to Josiah, it confirmed in writing what he knew to be true. So what does this twenty-something king do? He gathers the leaders and all the people together at the house of the Lord to read them The Book. After he finished,

> The king stood in his place and made a covenant before the LORD, to walk after the LORD and to keep his commandments and his testimonies and his statutes, with all his heart and all his soul, to perform the words of the covenant that were written in this book.[2]

In it all, the Lord responds to Josiah's humility and obedience with a promise for his later years:

> Behold, I will gather you to your fathers, and you shall be gathered to your grave in peace.[3]

As Josiah read The Book, it became a journey of discovery, which would consume the rest of his life. As I read in print what happened, I am stirred by his passion. It thrills me! The only thing better would be to hear his voice speaking of the day he first touched The Book. If he could talk to me, I would be reading a walking book. That too would be a journey of discovery. What an adventure. In Emily Dickinson's words: "There is no frigate like a book to take you lands away!"[4]

WRITTEN BOOKS AND WALKING BOOKS

We have two kinds of books in our lives: written books and walking books. One is "off the shelf" and the other is "in the flesh." It is worth noting that when dictators want to destroy a culture, they jail the clergy and academics and burn their books. They get rid of two wellsprings of ideas at the same time: the walking one and the printed one. And therein lies a tale.

I had just finished speaking at the university chapel service, and the director of student life said, "A number of students would like to chat with you informally for a bit. Do you have time?" I did. So several dozen of us congregated on the lawn in front of the library. The setting overlooking the Pacific Ocean was lovely, and the questions were good.

"What are some of the favorite books in your library, Mr. Foth?" I named a few. Then, surprising myself, I said, "I actually have two libraries. One of them is full of written, published books, like the library behind us. You check out a book, read it, and return it in two weeks.

"The other library I have is sitting next to you. These are in-the-flesh books. They have passion and energy and spontaneity. Their words have tone and volume and intensity. They are dynamic and always changing. These are interactive books that talk to you and you don't need to return them."

I went on to say that in writing papers, we cite passages from printed books in the bibliography. Those citations are called secondary resources. If, however, we interview someone for the paper, that is called a primary resource. Why? Because the power of a first-person-telling has an intimacy and punch that a written account two or three times removed cannot capture.

A Surprise Walking Book

The eighty-year-old man sitting in the back of the room was auditing the history class at a university in Southern California. The topic for the hour was D-day, June 6, 1944, on the Normandy beaches. As the teacher set the stage, she cited various authors describing that day, about which war correspondent Andy Rooney later wrote,

> There have been only a handful of days since the beginning
> of time on which the direction the world was taking has been
> changed for the better in one twenty-four-hour period by an
> act of man. June 6, 1944, was one of them.[5]

The teacher went on to give more details. Over five thousand Allied vessels of all kinds from battleships with sixteen-inch guns to Higgins landing crafts with no real armament stretched from the surf line to the far horizon of the English Channel. It was the largest naval armada ever assembled. Hundreds of landing crafts had to plow through rough seas, some from over ten miles out. Almost every man was sick as they approached the beaches.

As the teacher began to tell the story, suddenly the old man raised his hand and said, "Excuse me. But that's not exactly how I remember it." With that, thirty faces turned toward him. *Here* was the real story. *This* was first person. *This* was the *walking book*.

How Do You Read a Walking Book?

She was a smallish woman with a quiet, commanding presence. How she taught changed my life. With a PhD from New York University, Dr. Lois LeBar led the Christian Education program at Wheaton College Graduate School in Illinois in 1964. Her calm presence, passion for teaching, and nudging questions opened the world to me in a fresh way.

She introduced me to a group of her friends: a set of questions known as the Six Honest Serving Men, which she quoted from the first stanza of a Rudyard Kipling poem:

> I keep six honest serving men
> (They taught me all I knew);
> Their names are What and Why and When
> And How and Where and Who.[6]

Those questions were her template for open-ended conversation.

She was a fifty-seven-year-old single professor, and I was a twenty-two-year-old married student, so we had little in common from the outside. Yet I could sense her deep love for Jesus and her appropriate love for me because of the kind of probing questions she asked, the time she took, and her unwillingness to let me settle for easy answers. Always gentle and always direct, her teaching approach was a turning point for how I do what I do to this day. She always engaged me in meaningful conversation. Years later, I read what philosopher and educator Mortimer Adler said about conversation: "Love without conversation is impossible," and I said to myself, *That's how Dr. Lois made me feel—loved on the educational journey.*

Her premise as a teacher was that if you wish to have a real in-depth conversation, stay away from questions that can be answered with *yes* or *no,* because the answers to those questions would be periods, not commas. For discovery, for learning, for growth, the conversation needs to keep going. And that's where the Six Honest Serving Men came in.

Questions We Ask While Walking

Open, honest conversation has a profusion of questions and responses, interruptions, and talking at the same time. Still the reading of the walking book works best with questions. All kinds of questions. Personal history questions. People-who-shaped-your-life questions. What-are-some-of-your-favorite-places? questions. What-did-you-do-for-fun-as-a kid? questions.

Nonthreatening personal questions help me. When you ask me about my past, as opposed to my current career for example, I feel much safer. I can pick and choose my answers with some level of ease. When you ask me right out of the chute, "What do you do?" and I have just lost my job, that's not comfortable for either of us.

"Where are you from originally?" is an easy place to start because it flows easily into *who* and *how* and *why* and *what* and *when.* When you ask me that question or any variations, like "Where were you born and brought up?" or "When did your people come to this country?" you allow me to explore where parents and grandparents came from. In a day when discovering family roots is all the rage on TV programs and determining ethnicity through a DNA sample is becoming more popular by the day, the story can be quite stimulating. Assuming, of course, that I want to learn by reading walking books. Learning is the key. Understanding another person is the by-product.

Some of us don't want to ask or be asked those kinds of questions. Pain surfaces too quickly. Perhaps we ping-ponged through a foster system or grew up in an orphanage. *Be gentle* is the operative phrase. You're dealing with my story. I didn't choose it, but I lived it. I may not have liked it, but it's one of the lenses through which I see the world. And it is valuable for you to know where I came from and at least passed through. My responses may not be articulate or in sequence, but they will be real. We are one-of-a-kind walking books and have good things to add to lives of those listening. Perhaps best of all, in a competitive world, when others ask to hear our stories, it is the one place we always get an A. Before we start, we have an A. In the middle, we have an A. When we are done, we still have an A. Who wouldn't want that kind of affirmation?

Some folks just have a gift for moving the story along by describing their roots. Rick Bragg, Pulitzer Prize–winning author and professor of journalism at the University of Alabama, is one of those. Ruth found him in a thrift shop in Falls Church, Virginia, a few years back. Well, not exactly him, but a book he had written based on the life of his mother called *All Over but the Shoutin'*. As we lay in bed that evening reading before we went to sleep, as we do most every night, Ruth said, "Wow! This is writing. You have to read this!" I did. The opening paragraphs of chapter 1 painted a picture of the place his parents were born. It took my breath away.

My mother and father were born in the most beautiful place
on earth in the foothills of the Appalachians along the
Alabama-Georgia line. It was a place where gray mists hid the
tops of low, deep green mountains, where redbone and bluetick

hounds flashed through the pines as they chased possums into the sacks of old men in frayed overalls, where old women in bonnets dipped Bruton snuff and hummed "Faded Love and Winter Roses" as they shelled purple hulls, canned peaches and made biscuits too good for this world. It was a place where playing the church piano loud was near as important as playing it right, where fearless young men steered long, black Buicks loaded with yellow whiskey down roads the color of dried blood, where the first frost meant hog killin' time and the mouthwatering smell of cracklin's would drift for acres from giant, bubbling pots.[7]

I could see it all. His words put me right there. And I'm a city guy from Oakland, California, who's never seen a bluetick hound or tasted cracklin's.

The only thing I wanted more than *reading* those words was *hearing* them. So I went on YouTube and listened to Rick Bragg tell stories. Loved it. The only thing better than *that* would be a real live conversation with *the walking book*. I have questions, you see . . .

I Read Walking Books and I Am a Walking Book

Back to questions for a minute. Questions are at the heart of discovery. That's true of science. It is true of leadership. It is true of the law. It is true of faith. And it is true of relationships. The willingness to ask questions and respond to them is the seedbed for any relationship.

The old adage "When you're talkin', you ain't learnin'" is accurate. Questions are to relationships what trowels and brushes are to the archaeologist on a dig. Every part of that exploration informs the larger picture. Unlike an archaeological site, I am alive and breathing and growing. I must invite you to explore my world. I control the process. So be aware and be gentle.

When you ask me my opinion on a matter or my feelings on a subject, I am honored. But when you ask me about my roots or family or education, I begin to believe you might actually want to know me. If, indeed, I am a walking book with sections and chapters and paragraphs and key ideas, then your inquiry turns the pages. When you begin to read, each page has its own dynamic. Each chapter reflects an episode or a season. And the early chapters inform the later chapters.

A few years ago, I was introduced to a process called the Life Plan. With the one-on-one help of a facilitator, it's a two-day, in-depth look at one's history, personality, gifts, skills, and dreams. The point is to help plan your trajectory going forward. So I decided to complete it with my friend Jeff, who's great at this stuff.

When I awoke that morning ready to get after it, Ruth began to chuckle. When I asked her why she was laughing, she said, "I think it's hilarious that a seventy-one-year-old man wants to do a Life Plan." I said, "Hey, hey! I could have thirty years left. I need a plan to know where I want to go and what I want to do!" One of the results of that two-day adventure is this book.

The heart of the Life Plan was two days of reflection led by nudges ("Tell me about your earliest memories with your family") and inquiry ("Who was the greatest influence on your thinking as a teenager?"). It wasn't counseling. It wasn't therapy. It wasn't psychoanalysis. It was pure and simple storytelling.

Family lore was told of great-uncles and hilarious aunts who made family gatherings real. I told Jeff about my great-grandparents, who came west in covered wagons. With my Scots-Irish roots, there might have been a wee bit of myth and fancy thrown in, but I told the stories as I remembered them. Trips taken and people encountered all mixed in with the highs and lows of seventy-plus trips around the sun. He helped me put words to the pieces of my life.

As I talked, he wrote and asked follow-up questions. On the second day, when I walked into the room, my story was hanging on the wall. Written and charted on large pieces of butcher paper, I saw my journey. Turning points, ups and downs, things of inconsequence and consequence, replete with spiritual watershed moments—they were all there in black-on-beige, the summation of my years.

I don't quite know why, but when I looked at my life-on-the-wall, tears welled hot behind my eyes. Over those two days, I had been the walking book, read and known.

It felt like coming home.

9

A Journal and a Velcro Ribbon

> My story is not important because it is mine,
> God knows, but because if I tell it anything like
> right, the chances are you will recognize that in
> many ways it is also yours.
>
> —Frederick Buechner, *Telling Secrets*

Ice and snow blasted the cockpit windows of the bombers, as the lead pilot scrambled for a place to land. It was January 1943. Two hours earlier twenty-one B-17s had taken off from Wendover Army Air Base in Utah, bound for England to enter the fight. But for the moment, they were fighting a blizzard over central Nebraska.

As they dropped low out of the storm, toward corn-stubbled fields, they saw an airfield. Well, not *exactly* an airfield. It was a makeshift airstrip on a farm, and none of the pilots knew if they could pull off the landing. Twenty of the planes made it. One crash-landed. The two hundred young crewmen, with .45 Colts strapped on their hips, climbed out of their planes and dropped onto the frozen ground and huddled together. As wind and snow whipped their faces, vehicle lights appeared in the distance. It was a convoy of cars and pickups. The citizens of North Platte, Nebraska, had arrived.

John Weldon, one of the navigators, described that experience to Ruth and me sixty years later, as we rocketed across Nebraska on the California Zephyr in an early February dawn. He and his spouse had gotten on the train somewhere west of Chicago during the night, and we had been seated with them in the dining car for breakfast. From the first sip of coffee it became clear that John had lived quite the life! We were being made privy to some pages from his old journal—a journal stained with sweat and blood and cherished over the years.

A JOURNAL OF LIFE

I am a journaling failure. I have a dozen journals in my study, each with a few weeks' worth of notations in them. I admire those who journal well. Authors like David McCullough who write of historical figures (*Truman* and *John Adams*) and Doris Kearns Goodwin *(Team of Rivals)* read personal letters and journals to discover the thoughts and feelings of the persons about whom they write. Journals are intimate. They are places we deposit what we know, think, and feel. They reveal who we are and what we value. Dan Allender elaborated on that:

> Our ideal self is revealed in what we value (passion), how we understand the world (belief), and what we do to reach our ideal (behavior). Our passion, belief, and behavior fit together so intimately that I can say this with confidence:
> - What we do is what we really value.
> - What we value enough to do tells others what we really believe.
> - What we really believe shapes what we will become.[1]

But the up-close, personal details of our lives are actually walking journals. When I tell you of a critical event in my life, it's a page from my journal. When I disclose a tension that is still unresolved, it's a page from my journal. Journals are powerful because they offer the two things so many of us crave: *authenticity* and *vulnerability*. At our core, we desire what is real. We don't want our lives altered like a document in Photoshop.

The old adage "Life is what happens when you're busy making other plans" kept ringing in my head as John talked with us on that train. Early in our conversation, I had simply asked, "By any chance, were you in World War II?" He took it from there. He shared with us that he finally got to England and flew eight missions. The first ended with a crash landing in the English Channel, with the whole crew rescued by the Royal Air Force within range of German guns on the Normandy coast. The eighth one ended with the crew bailing out over Czechoslovakia and spending the next twenty-one months in a POW camp.

He told me that by the end of the war their guards were young teenage boys, who didn't want to be there any more than the prisoners did. Some of them became friends. He'd never forget the day he stood talking with one of them. On hearing the sound of tanks, they looked up to see some of General George Patton's Spearhead Tenth Armored Division rolling up on the far side of the river. The young guard turned, handed John his machine gun, then just walked off into the woods.

I have eaten thousands of breakfasts in my lifetime, but breakfast that morning in an Amtrak dining car will stand as one of the most moving conversations I have ever been party to.

John's candor in the telling of his story drew us in.

He didn't just tell us the good parts. He told of the fear when they were shot down and captured, then marched to the stalag past what looked like ordinary factories with chimneys belching smoke, only later to learn they were death camps. The fear of starving was always there. They had no reason to believe they would ever see home again. We, of course, had never come close to experiencing what John had, but we had known fear. We had known our own kind of suffering. Truth be told, we identify more readily with suffering than we do with victories. Victories are unique. Suffering is universal.

We talked all through breakfast, and he asked if we'd join them for lunch. When lunch was concluded, he said, "Dick, before we leave, could you say one of those open-eyed prayers with us?" I had told him earlier about a lawyer I prayed with one time who did so with one caveat: "I don't close my eyes!" Worked for me!

With people walking past us in the narrow aisle and waiters serving lunches, we talked to the Creator of the Universe. The distance from a death camp to a dining car is the time it takes to offer up a few journal pages from a rich life. John's vulnerability made it possible. He didn't try to hide who he was, and it made him real. It reminded me of some words Ruth wrote years ago about playing dress-up:

Playing dress-up again—just like a kid,
With clothes that don't fit,
Shoes that are too big
And a hat that covers my eyes.
Just a harmless little disguise,

I think. But the longer it's worn,
Not only does it hide me from you,
I no longer recognize myself.

A VELCRO RIBBON

When you share parts of the journal of your life, it becomes a Velcro ribbon to which another person can attach. They can connect with places, people, and experiences. They identify with your challenges and your pain. Scripture is full of journal entries. Listen to Luke's account of Jesus's birth:

In those days Caesar Augustus issued a decree that a census should be taken of the entire Roman world. (This was the first census that took place while Quirinius was governor of Syria.) And everyone went to his own town to register.

So Joseph also went up from the town of Nazareth in Galilee to Judea, to Bethlehem the town of David, because he belonged to the house and line of David. He went there to register with Mary, who was pledged to be married to him and was expecting a child. While they were there, the time came for the baby to be born, and she gave birth to her firstborn, a son. She wrapped him in cloths and placed him in a manger, because there was no room for them in the inn.[2]

The whole scenario revolves around a dictator doing what dictators do: *they take your money and sometimes your life.* We're told the name of the governor, and we know that the Mary-and-Joseph-Bethlehem-trip was to please the Roman equivalent of the Census Bureau. But the tax shekels were small potatoes compared to the other thing: they were only *engaged* and *she* was already pregnant. In their culture, that was a dead-end road. *That* was the real trip.

Jesus was born in a cave in the middle of the night attended by sheep, shepherds, and singing angels. A while later, King Herod, upset about another king in town, decided it's killing time. Which means the new family had to run for it.

If we are political leaders, engaged couples, or unwed moms, we connect to this story. If we come from poverty, live on sheep ranches, have been in danger not of our own making, or found ourselves refugees, we connect to this story. *It's a Velcro ribbon.*

Two thousand years later and six thousand miles away, I stand in a five-star hotel about as far as one can get from a Middle East stable. We are doing small-group things with leaders from Japan, the United States, Canada, India, and Russia. My co-leader asks me a simple question, "Where were you born, Dick?" and I reply, "Alameda, California." At that moment, a Japanese man to my far right speaks up, in perfect English, "Isn't that near Oakland?" "Why, yes. How do you know that?" He replies, "That's where IBM trained me." When the session finishes, he makes a beeline for me. It turns out I was speaking to the president of IBM Japan. *It's a Velcro ribbon.*

RISK AND REWARD

To be vulnerable is to risk. To be authentic is to tell the truth unvarnished. Ruth and I met Charles Greenaway in the 1960s. A longtime missionary in Africa and Europe, he was a consummate storyteller with the gift for challenging listeners to go and do and give. If you asked him, "How're you doing, Charles?" his response would always be, "Gonna make it! Not gonna look like much when I get there, but I'm gonna make it!"

One day I said, "Charles, when did you start saying 'Gonna make it?'" And he told me this story:

I was brought up in the coalfields of Pennsylvania during the Depression. They were terrible times. Families were large and poor and sometimes children would have to be sent to state-run orphanages because the families couldn't handle one more mouth to feed.

I'll not forget the day my daddy died. His body was laid out on the table in our small house. I was just a little guy, and as my brother and I stood by that table with my mom, she said, "Charlie, don't you worry—we're gonna stay together." But something happened over the next year. I don't know what. And one day she sat me down and said, "Charlie, I'm so sorry, but you're gonna need to go to a home for a while. I'll come and get you as soon as I can." I didn't hear anything else she said because the birds stopped singing, the band stopped playing, and the lights went out.

I'll never forget the day the man from the orphanage came to get me. Pulling up in a black Ford Model T he wore a bowler hat and had a big cigar clenched between his teeth. I was hiding around the corner of the house, when he stepped into our little front yard. He just stood there and said, "Well . . .

where is he?" Like I was a side of meat. My knees knocking together, I came out from my hiding place and went and stood in front of him. Scared to death.

The next thing I knew, I felt the warmth of my mother's body next to me, as her arm slipped around my shoulders in a fierce grip. She looked that man in the eye and said, "Mister, I've changed my mind. Charlie ain't goin'. We're gonna make it!" The lights came on, the birds started singing, and the band started playing. It was the greatest day of my life!

Apart from the tears in my eyes and a lump the size of a baseball in my throat, I was so struck by the plain vulnerability of the story that it has stayed with me for all these years. The Great Depression seared certain values into that generation. They valued small things and worked unceasingly their whole lives. Many of those young men never had a new pair of shoes until they enlisted in the army in World War II. And they saw leadership in a simple way. At least, Charles did.

Over lunch one day, I asked him a leadership question.

I said, "Charles, what's your philosophy of leadership?"

He said, "Simple, Dick. Protect the person above you and protect the person below you and everything works."

I said, "That's it?"

He said, "Oh, one more thing. If you ever cross me, there is no redemption."

Stunned, I stammered, "But that doesn't sound very biblical!"

He grinned and said, "Oh, I don't think it is. It came out of the Depression. If you didn't stay together, if you weren't loyal to each other, you died."

I'm not espousing Charles's philosophy. I was just touched by his authenticity. He didn't try to say he was right. He simply told me the truth of his experience. He put it out there. I could make my own judgment. Friends do that. They try to understand. Then they argue and scrap and try to convince, because the relationship matters.

GETTING SCARRED, FEELING TRAPPED

Sometimes we don't want to expose parts of our lives because we have scars from wounds, some of which may still be tender. We are embarrassed by them or afraid to try to explain the pieces. No one's journey is a straight line. No story is without travail. Pat Conroy, in *Beach Music,* said it beautifully:

> No story is a straight line. The geometry of a human life is too
> imperfect and complex, too distorted by the laughter of time
> and the bewildering intricacies of fate to admit the straight line
> into its system of laws.[3]

The truth is, if we are looking for someone without scars, we are living on the wrong planet. Everyone has scars. Jesus has scars. Maybe especially he has scars. He uses those scars to prove his humanity and start the restoration journey for his frightened and sometime-believing disciples. Scars aren't bad. They just tell you where you don't want to go again.

The other fear we have is that we are trapped by our history. I know people who live believing that lie. And they *are* trapped. But Jesus has come to unlock our doors and let us out. We don't need to be trapped by our history, but we are absolutely shaped by our history. Every experience has left an imprint. That's why to read through that journal and share it with another is so revealing and freeing. That's why taking that chance is worth it.

Over the years, I have reflected on some thoughts by Ernest L. Stech that put the authentic, the vulnerable, friendship, and God all in the same room:

> That's my soul lying there.
> You don't know what a soul is?
> You think it's some kind of ghostly sheet-like thing you
>   can see through and it floats in the air?
> That's my soul lying there
> Remember when my hand shook because I was nervous
>   in the group?
> Remember the night I goofed and argued too much and
>   got mad and couldn't get out of the whole mess?
> I was putting my soul on the line.
> Another time I said that someone once told me some-
>   thing about herself that she didn't have to.
> I said that she told me something that could have hurt her.
> And I guess I was asking you to do the same.
> I was asking you to let me know you.
> That's part of my soul, too.
> When I told you that my mother didn't love my dad and
>   I knew it as a kid,
> When I said that my eyes water when I get hurt even
>   though I'm thirty-four and too much a man to cry,

I was putting my soul out there in the space between you
        and me.
Yeah, that's my soul lying there.
I've never met God.
I mean I've never met that old man who sits on a cloud with
        a crown and a staff and knows everything and is
        everything and controls everything.
But I've met you.
Is that God in your face?
Is that God in your soul lying there?
Well, that's my soul lying there.
I'll let you pick it up.
That's why I put it there.
It'll bruise and turn rancid like an old banana if you want
        to manhandle it.
It'll go away if you want to ignore it.
But if you want to put your soul there beside it, there may
        be love.
There may even be God.[4]

I've read those words for decades, yet they still move me. The risk
and reward of authentic, vulnerable living is worth it a hundred times
over. When we take a chance and offer a page of our journal to be read
by another, something happens that happens no other way. Why is
that? It's the risk-and-reward principle and, even biology, in play.

In a culture of scarcity and perfectionism, there's a surprisingly
simple reason we want to own, integrate, and share our stories

of struggle. We do this because we feel the most alive when we're connecting with others and being brave with our stories—it's in our biology. . . . Neuroeconomist Paul Zak has found that hearing a story—a narrative with a beginning, middle, and end—causes our brains to release cortisol and oxytocin. These chemicals trigger the uniquely human abilities to connect, empathize, and make meaning. Story is literally in our DNA.[5]

What a gift each of us holds in the owning and telling of our stories, the sharing of our journal pages with other people. No other person on the planet or in all of human history has what you cradle uniquely in your head and heart.

Frederick Buechner sure got it:

Maybe nothing is more important than that we keep track, you and I, of these stories of who we are and where we have come from and the people we have met along the way because it is precisely through these stories in all their particularity, as I have long believed and often said, that God becomes known to each of us most powerfully and personally.

If this is true, it means that to lose track of our stories is to be profoundly impoverished not only humanly, but also spiritually.[6]

If the original premise of this book is true, that we deal with money and relationships our whole lives and it's the relationships not money that make us rich, let's be sure we don't end up impoverished.

Let's read another page of that journal. Just turn to the page where you stopped.

You know, the place marked by the Velcro ribbon.

RUTH'S THOUGHTS

The first time I looked at her little face, I lost my heart to her. I wanted to hold her, protect her, and spend as much time with her as I could. Alyson was our first grandchild. And it was then I knew I had made the right decision. During those cold days of the preceding December, we held a secret close to us that warmed us, one that would change our lives. We were going to become grandparents. And for this child I would do something to keep us close, even when we lived far apart. I would keep a journal of our days together.

If you have grandchildren, you understand. There really aren't words to describe the moment you first see that little baby that is your child's child—the beginning of a new generation. It isn't just pride or catch-your-breath-love or joy. It's all of these and more! And you begin wanting to capture the moments you have together.

When our own children were young, I was in survival mode and there weren't enough hours in the day. Today, when my grandchildren ask me what their parents were like when they were young, I'm often at a loss for words. I know I've forgotten many special moments, ones I thought at the time I had cataloged in my brain. Now I wish I had taken time to write some things down. Why is it that those years seem overwhelmingly long when you're living them but are over in a flash as you look back?

I determined to be more intentional as a grandmother. I wouldn't let memories with my grandchildren slip away. I would record them. Each time we had a visit I would record their likes and dislikes, their interests, their growth, and what we did together. And I would keep the artwork they sent and their photos. Then when they were young adults, I would compile everything in a little book and present it to them.

Alyson was born in Eugene, Oregon. We got to be in the hospital waiting room. We held her in our arms just minutes after her birth. I thought she was the most beautiful baby I had ever seen. Dick and I made the trip from our home in California to Oregon as often as we could. When her parents moved near us, we were with her every week. Then we moved to North Carolina.

That's when my journaling began to play a more important role in our relationship. I wanted Aly to know that even if we lived far away, she was always in my thoughts. The words in her journal came easily because I was recounting my impressions of our special times together. I recorded all the amusing and wonderful things she did when she came to visit, because this was a priority.

My task grew as other grandchildren were born. From the date we learned of their impending arrival, I began writing. For many, I got to be with their parents when they were born. For some, it was shortly afterward. Each one was wonderfully different.

When Aly was a teenager, I asked her when she would like to have a copy of her journal. She told me, "When I graduate from high school." So that became my goal. I would combine my writing with her pieces of art, her awards at school, and photos of her I had been collecting. The journal would be my gift to her when she graduated from high school.

Since then, I have given our second granddaughter, Claire, her journal. Sam, our first grandson, is next on the list. It's fun for me to read through the journal pages I've kept and reminisce about all the times we've had together—chapters of their lives that give me pause to be grateful for them and to pray for God's continued guidance in their lives. Prayer seems to go right along with journaling.

I see keeping these journals as a way to encourage our grandchildren and a special way to keep that relational tie between us strong. We want them to know that their stories are important to us, that we are honored to be part of their lives, and that we love and know them, not only as grandchildren, but as friends.

AFFIRMERS

Hearing Your Story, I
Learn How to Love You

10

Speaking to God

Therefore *encourage one another* and build each
other up, just as in fact you are doing.

—1 Thessalonians 5:11

The smiling young mom said, "Eric has something he wants to tell you."

The ten-year-old boy and his mother had been standing off to my right waiting to see me after my talk. As I turned toward them, she made that statement. I gave him a knuckle bump and said, "Great! What's happening, Eric?" He looked me in the eye and said, "I really liked your talk. You did good."

That was it! There's the Oscar. That's Olympic gold. We are inching up on the Presidential Medal of Freedom. When a ten-year-old tells a seventy-year-old that he actually listened and got it? Ring the bells and fire the cannons. The old guy can die happy!

Affirmation is a four-dollar word that means "I like you!" It permeates the fabric of a friendship, and without it, friendships don't work. Coming in myriad forms, it is a baseline for hope and provides stability. When you are friends, affirming the other is way high on the intuitive scale. Let's call that scale the Reflex Quotient (RQ), the things that one does naturally. Affirmation tops the list on the RQ Index.

The question is, How do you affirm someone in a way that will be received? Personalities are all over the map. We are wired in unique ways. Some of us respond to spoken words. Others respond to deeds or written words. And on the list goes. So let's look at five concrete ways of affirming.

SPEAKING TO GOD

When I pulled my brand-new Vespa scooter into our front yard on Congress Avenue in east Oakland, California, on that November afternoon, I had my standard expectation: snacks at the hand of my stay-at-home mom. What I got when I walked in was no mom and no snacks. The house was silent.

If you have been brought up with a theology that the Second Coming of Jesus Christ could happen at any moment, a disappeared mother is not a good sign. Our 1920s stucco bungalow wasn't big, so I quickly covered most of the rooms inside and headed down the short hall toward my folks' bedroom. That's when I heard the noise. It was coming from the small walk-in closet in their room.

Creeping up to the door, I was able to decipher the muffled sounds from down near the floor. It was a mother on her knees praying for a wayward son. Really? I wasn't *that* wayward. Sure, I was a seventeen-year-old freshman at Cal Berkeley, but I came from a highly structured, conservative religious family. Perhaps I *was* sowing some wild oats. But by twenty-first-century standards there weren't many oats and they weren't very wild! Anyway, Mom was talking to God in classic fashion: "Oh, God, don't let Dick do anything more stupid than he's already done!" For the most part, it worked.

My takeaway from that day was not that my mom was fervent in prayer but that my mom cared enough for me that she would get on her knees in a closet in the middle of the day to bring my name and need before the Creator of the Universe and invoke his help. Now, *that's* affirmation.

Prayer cuts through arguments, crosses all the lines of bias, and soothes the wounded soul. It invokes the help of Another in strengthening your hands, healing your heart, and giving you hope. No other action we take can do what prayer does.

Ruth lay in an induced coma at the Medical Center of the Rockies in Loveland. She had been that way for thirty-six hours, when a doctor we didn't really know walked into room 2B in the Cardiac Intensive Care Unit. He introduced himself as a cardiac surgeon making nightly rounds. It was 10 p.m.

The morning before and an hour away at 8,000 feet in the Rockies, Ruth had collapsed. The EMTs called it "sudden cardiac death" caused by ventricular heart arrhythmia. Survival rate nationally outside a hospital is just 6 percent, and 11 percent for those resuscitated in the field. Of those, just a few survive without some brain function impact. The doctors who initially treated her simply said to us, "We have no idea what you can expect by way of function when she wakes up. If she wakes up."

The surgeon who had walked into the ICU looked around and said, "Dick, I have a sense this is going to be all right." As far as I could tell, there was no empirical data to support that statement. Then he asked, "May I pray for Ruth?" I've been in scores of hospitals in my life and dozens of ICUs. Not once has a doctor asked me that question. I said, "Absolutely!" At that point, with nurses and technicians moving about, he laid his hand on her and in a strong voice began to pray, "Lord, God, Almighty . . ."[1] Four hours later, Ruth woke up. Nine days later, she left the hospital with no negative cognitive function. Three years later, we are writing this book together.

You ask, "Did that prayer do the trick?" Certainly. That prayer and the incredible skills of a highly competent medical team did the trick. What that prayer did precisely in terms of healing I don't know, but I believe it had a part. That was a prayer for Ruth and I got the overflow. What that prayer did was to let me know that God knew where we were. What that prayer did was to affirm the innate value of a seventy-one-year-old woman who had taken a massive physical hit and lay intubated in the space between life and death. What that prayer did was absolutely 100 percent positive. What an affirmation!

PRAYER IS THE HIGHEST AFFIRMATION

It is words to God. When you pray for a person, it is you talking to God about another. Let's be very clear: Your prayer does not *create* that person's value. It *acknowledges* that person's value. Prayer for another person says this: "I believe you are so valuable that I'd like to bring your needs and you by name to the Creator of the Universe when I speak with him this afternoon!" Your prayer affirms the Grand Design. Your prayer affirms God's ongoing interest and engagement in the life of that person. Your prayer affirms value even in negative circumstances.

One of my favorite characters in the Gospels is Simon Peter. A strong, natural leader with big arms and a big mouth, Simon Peter is a fixer and a protector. Problem is, he often promises more than he can produce. His mouth runs away with him. All that is changed, of course, on the Day of Pentecost when the Holy Spirit fills him up with fresh insights and real boldness. But before that, his batting average is not so good. He has swings and misses aplenty! He is strong in some ways and weak in others. Maybe that's why I identify with him. As Jesus heads toward his certain death, he says something very interesting to Simon Peter:

> Simon, Simon, behold, Satan demanded to have you, that
> he might sift you like wheat, but I have prayed for you that
> your faith may not fail. And when you have turned again,
> strengthen your brothers.[2]

He knows what's coming for Simon; he will have the best of intentions and the worst of responses. At the moment of greatest challenge, he will fail. It fascinates me that Jesus, knowing what's coming down, doesn't say, "Here, let me tell you how to avoid that!" Instead he says, "I have prayed for you that your faith may not fail." In other words, "You might fail in the moment, but your faith will win out in the long haul. And by the way, I'm speaking to my Father about you." Prayer cuts down and through and across every circumstance.

ALL OF US NEED PRAYER

During our fifteen years in Washington, DC, talking with scores of men and women in high and low places, I was encouraged by my mentors to ask this question somewhere in a conversation—usually toward the end: "I have friends who believe that praying for leaders is important. Is there anything I can ask them to pray for?" Not once in all those years did any of the individuals say no. I've asked myself many times, *Why were they all, to a person, willing to receive prayer?* I think it's because we all desire the interest and affirmation of the Most High. Even if someone doesn't believe in him, they intuitively cover their bets.

Tony Blair, former Prime Minister of Britain, speaking at the 2009 National Prayer Breakfast, told a story about his father:

> I remember my first spiritual awakening. I was ten years old.
> That day my father—at the young age of 40—had suffered a
> serious stroke. His life hung in the balance. My mother, to keep
> some sense of normality in the crisis, sent me to school. My
> teacher knelt and prayed with me. Now my father was a
> militant atheist. Before we prayed, I thought I should confess
> this. "I'm afraid my father doesn't believe in God," I said. "That
> doesn't matter," my teacher replied, "God believes in him. He
> loves him without demanding or needing love in return."[3]

Prayer, as an affirmation, counts on the fact that a loving God believes in us. It affirms who *God* is and who *we* are all at one shot! So when the apostle Paul prayed, "I want to *know* Christ," it was a prayer for himself. It was the place of beginning from which all his other relationships develop.[4]

It is fascinating to see the relationships then that Paul developed in the first century as he made his way on foot across the northern edge of the Mediterranean Basin three times in three years. From Antioch in Syria, he headed southwest to Cyprus and then up to places in present-day Turkey, like Antalya, Perga, Iconium, Lystra, and Derby. On his second trip, he went to Philippi, Tarsus, Thessalonica, Derbe, Beroea, Lystra, Athens, Iconium, Corinth, Troas, and Ephesus. The third trip, he didn't go new places. He circled back to see old friends. One of those cities was Philippi.

When he wrote his friends in Philippi later, he started with a big dose of encouragement:

I thank my God every time I remember you. In all my prayers for all of you, I always pray with joy because of your partnership in the gospel from the first day until now, being confident of this, that he who began a good work in you will carry it on to completion until the day of Christ Jesus.

It is right for me to feel this way about all of you, since I have you in my heart; for whether I am in chains or defending and confirming the gospel, all of you share in God's grace with me. God can testify how I long for all of you with the affection of Christ Jesus.

And this is my prayer: that your love may abound more and more in knowledge and depth of insight, so that you may be able to discern what is best and may be pure and blameless until the day of Christ, filled with the fruit of righteousness that comes through Jesus Christ—to the glory and praise of God.[5]

After his initial greeting, it is right there: "I thank my God every time I remember you. In all my prayers for all of you, I always pray with joy." Under any conditions, prayer is a great affirmation. But when you have survived an earthquake in a town, eaten in people's homes, introduced the local jailer and his family to Jesus, and helped start a congregation, that's a different deal. You know their story. And when you know a person's story—*where* his or her journey has taken them—you know *where* to affirm them.

A mother can do that. A doctor can do that. A teacher can do that. A spiritual parent can do that.

You and I can do that!

RUTH'S THOUGHTS

Because both my father and my husband were pastors, I've been in church nearly every Sunday of my life. Coming from Pentecostal roots, I was brought up in services that were exuberant and spontaneous. When Dick attended Wheaton College Grad School, I came to appreciate the ordered chapel services we attended with pipe organ music and the singing of old hymns of the church. But I wasn't sure what to expect that Sunday morning.

I walked up the steps and through the tall Greek columns of Commonwealth Chapel with my good friend Joan. She and I and our husbands had spent ten years in the Washington, DC, area. Our friendship had grown over those years, while we spent time together and learned we enjoyed many of the same things—reading good books, finding great buys at thrift shops and nurturing our grandkids. Since then, Joan had moved to Richmond, and I was there for a visit. On this particular Sunday, we chose to attend the church where her son was pastor. The chapel was built in 1905 in the historic Fan district of Richmond and had housed various congregations over the years. As we entered the sanctuary, I noted the beautiful stained glass window over the baptistery and a collection of candles in holders on the communion table.

I had a family situation troubling me that morning. The young pastor spoke to those assembled and most directly to me, it seemed. He asked those of us with a pressing need to come forward and offer our request to God by lighting a candle. I asked Joan to come with me, and we walked down the aisle together. After I lit a candle, we returned to our seats. I left that service with a lighter heart, feeling somehow that the burden I was carrying had shifted onto the shoulders of the Carpenter/Healer. He had heard my silent words, as I stood in the light of that candle. And, for me, the candle signified that moment and stood for that transfer.

When I returned home, I thought often about that simple act of faith and how meaningful it had been for me. And I decided that it didn't need to be confined to the sanctuary of a church. When I felt the strong desire to bring a friend to Christ in prayer, I could light a candle and set it on my kitchen counter—as a reminder to be in prayer. Each time I saw the flame, I would offer up a prayer to the One who understood and would certainly answer in his time and his way. Each time I saw the flame, I would remind myself that not only my prayers but also the collective prayers of all believers would come before the Heavenly Father.

I have a very large candle in a beautiful glass holder—the gift of a friend. It's my prayer candle. When it burns low, I make sure it gets replaced. Sometimes when a need seems overwhelming, I bring out several candles and light all of them. It's my way of saying, "Lord, I want you to know that this is a terribly big request. It's very important to me, and I don't know how in the world you will answer it . . . but please hear my prayers." I know he does. And I keep reminding myself that I don't have to figure out the answer. I don't even have to make some suggestions—though they sometimes sound pretty good to me. He knows the future and knows what's best.

When I faced death in the mountains of Estes Park, Colorado, many folks who knew my candle-lighting tradition began following my fight for life on Facebook. They started lighting candles and posting the pictures. One of my daughter's friends even lit a bonfire on an ocean beach in Virginia. The day when I experienced sudden cardiac death and several days after have been erased from my memory, but the stories that I hear about those days are overwhelming. It is incredible and so humbling to know that many, many people were praying for me—a great chorus of prayers to the Father of Life. The doctors say that I am a miracle. When I think of first responders, I know that the police, the firefighters, the paramedics, and the doctors all helped tremendously. But I had the huge advantage of being surrounded by friends in prayer from the moment I collapsed.

In reality, these friends were the very first responders.

The older I get, my prayer time has become more profound and a greater resource for me. I love knowing I can be in communion with Jesus all during the day—in times of great happiness and times of dire need. And I love knowing that I can be in touch with the divine when I'm completing the most ordinary tasks of my day—like cleaning bathrooms or pulling weeds in my garden. Any time with him is enriching and life giving. Of course there are times I need to find a quiet place where I can be alone, offer my requests to the Lord, and listen with my heart. Then I am reassured by the One "who is able to do exceedingly abundantly above all that we ask or think."[6]

And often that's when I light a candle.

11

Speaking to You

The right word at the right time is like a custom-made
piece of jewelry, and a wise friend's timely reprimand
is like a gold ring slipped on your finger.

—Proverbs 25:11–12, MSG

There's hardly anything better than a third-party affirmation. I don't know how many times it happened that we'd walk into that home on Carver Road in Modesto to see Ruth's parents sitting at the kitchen table. With a quick glance they'd see one of our kids with us, and the conversation would quickly shift into something like, "Mother, I was thinking about Chris just the other day." She'd respond, "Yes, Daddy, isn't he just the best!" That would continue for a few moments, then they would welcome all of us standing in the entryway.

That brief exchange within the hearing of a child makes the heart soar!

A WAY WITH WORDS

Words can be gifts or weapons. When they are gifts, our lives are never the same. When they are weapons, our lives are never the same. Language moves us to the heights or takes us to the depths. Going to the depths when you are angry with someone might feel like the way to go, but it can really come back to bite you.

For years, I kept a piece of free verse by Carl Sandburg on my desk. I did it because I sat in the chair of power. I wasn't responsible for thousands of people, but several hundred. Some would come to me for advice, counsel, and decisions. It is so easy when you sit in the catbird seat to wield authority for your own benefit, just because you can. In "Primer Lesson," Sandburg wrote:

> Look out how you use proud words.
> When you let proud words go, it is
> > not easy to call them back.
> They wear long boots, hard boots; they
> > walk off proud; they can't hear you calling—
> Look out how you use proud words.[1]

Proud words and friendship can't occupy the same space for very long. Sure, friends have disagreements. Sometimes they even fight, scrap, and come to loggerheads. But in the end, they come around and still like each other.

Encouraging words, challenging words, gentle words are the food of friendship. They can be direct or subtle, loud or soft, single words or sentences. But they will carry a tone that buoys the spirit. Words between friends can be jokes or soft sarcasm, which are okay if the tone is right. Studies have shown that about 80 percent of communication is not just found in words spoken but in the tone used.

THE TONE OF THE LANGUAGE

Some years ago, I walked into the house and said something to Ruth in a poor tone. I was young and excited and changing the whole world. Some younger people were actually following me, I thought. So, I must be pretty good! In that full-of-myself moment, I said something in a way that was offensive. The words were okay, but my tone was condescending.

Ruth's response was, "Do you know how it makes me feel when you use that tone with me?" I didn't know what using that tone did to this lovely woman, my best friend. I was the less for it. We were both the less for it.

Positive words with a positive tone are a tremendous gift. I love the story of Sally, a little girl who had been born with a cleft palate. As you can imagine, her self-image took a hit each time she looked in the mirror. Every year the teacher at her school conducted a hearing test in the class by having each student by turn go across the room and stand facing the door. She then would whisper a phrase to judge the acuity of the child's hearing.

The day came when it was Sally's turn to be tested and the teacher told her to go stand by the door and face away from her. The words Sally heard next were the most wonderful, life-changing words anyone had ever spoken to her. Her teacher simply whispered, "I wish you were my little girl."

Texts and e-mails with emojis and exclamation points can certainly convey positive thoughts and feelings. But nothing takes the place of what I hear in your voice. Your voice is one of a kind. I don't need spectrographic analysis to know the variations in your timbre and inflection. When you say, "Hello!" I know who it is.

Just a voice of calm or authority in a stressful moment can mean the world. Talking with a friend one day, a retired major general in the army, I said, "Bob, as you look back on your whole career, what is the one thing for which you are most grateful?" He thought a moment, then said, "That my men knew my voice in the dark."

That sounded like Jesus. He used all kinds of metaphors when he spoke of the relationship we have with him. They reflect his context: fields and laborers, vineyards and winepresses, fish and fishermen, tax collectors, religious types, and perhaps most particularly, shepherds and sheep. He is the Good Shepherd, and we are the sheep. This is how he described the interaction: "My sheep hear my voice, and I know them, and they follow me."[2] To *hear*, to *know*, and to *follow* are intimately connected.

Can you imagine the tone of Paul's voice when he affirmed his friends in Philippi in the introductory paragraphs of his letter? Listen to him:

> It is right for me to feel this way about you all, because I hold
> you in my heart, for you are all partakers with me of grace,
> both in my imprisonment and in the defense and confirmation
> of the gospel. For God is my witness, how I yearn for you all
> with the affection of Christ Jesus.[3]

His choice of words carries the emotion, even if we can't actually hear the tone. It is "right for me to feel this way!" "I hold you in my heart!" "How I yearn for you all!" I read these phrases and say to myself, *Is this the Paul I know from his story?*

Is this the Saul who "breathed threatening and slaughter" before he was transformed? Is this the Paul that faced down city leaders and authorities in place after place without fear and with great intensity? Is this the Paul who, when his apostolic authority was challenged in 2 Corinthians 11, called his accusers out by saying, "Okay, boys! Let's take off our shirts and compare scars from Roman cat-o'-nine-tails that we carry on our backs for the sake of the gospel. Then we can talk." Is this the let's-walk-across-Turkey-and-spend-time-in-their-jails guy?

What was he doing using language and tone so infused with feeling and hope? Simple. He was talking to friends. That's how friends do it. They affirm at every opportunity. They encourage and lift up. They challenge and reflect. Their words are gifts to be cherished and stored like treasures. They are life-whisperers.

ONE SENTENCE CAN CHANGE YOUR WORLD

When Ruth and I were becoming friends in the early 1960s, we attended college about eighty miles south of San Francisco near Santa Cruz. I had been a stutterer since my earliest British boarding school days in South India. Though I had learned to mask it in some ways and trigger speech in others, as many stutterers learn to do just to survive, it was a royal pain for me. I saw it as a noncommunicable social disease.

One evening as we drove down West Cliff Drive along the Pacific Ocean, I wanted to say to her, "I don't know if you want to keep going out with me, because I stutter." The words tumbled over each other with short pauses. She looked over at me, smiled sweetly, and said some great words: "Oh, really. I hadn't noticed." The jail door swung open. The antidote to the disease was injected. I can still hear the words and her lovely tone. Now *that's* what I'm talking about. *That's* a friend.[4]

WORDS THAT PAINT PICTURES

What amazes me is the speed with which positive words can change a tense atmosphere. Or how affirming language can transform someone's life. There were three hundred of us in the ballroom of the Holiday Inn in St. Louis, Missouri, participating in small-group training conducted by Serendipity Workshops back in the early 1970s. We had been placed randomly in small groups of six. The morning had been spent telling our stories. It's amazing how much you can learn about someone's history when the right kinds of questions are asked!

After lunch we reassembled according to this instruction: "Arrange five chairs in a horseshoe, then place the sixth chair inside the open end of the horseshoe. All six of you will take your turn in that sixth chair over the course of the next hour. It is there that the other five members of the group will take time to speak to you. On the basis of what you have learned about each other in the hours before this, you will be affirmed using positive phrases or in terms of a color or in terms of an animal. It will be positive, and all you can say is 'Thank you!'"

The first person in the affirmation chair was an eighteen-year-old boy. As we went around the horseshoe, you could see how much he was enjoying the things that were said, until we came to a young woman about his own age. She looked at him and said, "You remind me of a dog." He rolled his eyes and exclaimed, "Oh, great!"

Then she went on, "No, no, this is good. I have a dog at home—a golden cocker spaniel with big brown eyes like yours and I like to hold him on my lap and pet him." At that point the young man blurted out with a great laugh, "That's more like it!" It was a wonderful, hilarious moment.

Then it came time for a young woman to take the chair. She had received a negative critique in her first year on the job, and apparently her employer felt she could use the experiences provided by the Serendipity Day to improve her social skills. In short, she was there under duress. It was clear in her words, her tone, her body language, and her nervous chain smoking all morning long, that she'd rather be any place in the world other than with us doing this stuff.

Again we went around the horseshoe with affirmations. They were good words but limited in some ways because she hadn't given us much to work with in the morning—until we got to that same young woman with the golden cocker. That was a moment.

She looked at the woman in the affirmation chair and said, "I see you as the color of your dress." It was fall, and the dress was silky and full of color—golds, umbers, reds, and browns. "I see you as a warm and spontaneous person and those colors remind me of a fire in my fireplace at my home in Rockford, Illinois." She went on, "I would like to take you there on a snowy winter night and sit in front of the fire. We could eat popcorn and drink hot chocolate, and I could just get to know you!"

With that last phrase, the woman in the pretty dress dropped her cigarette on the tile floor and ground it out with her shoe.

Then she looked up at the girl and said, "Say that one more time!" The girl did.

By the time she finished, tears were streaming down the other woman's face as she forced out the words, "Nobody in my whole life has ever wanted to spend an evening with me just to get to know me!"

I don't know where that frustrated, angry woman went, the one conveying her displeasure at every turn. Because the woman we sat with the rest of the afternoon was delightful. A mature young girl's affirming words had unlocked her heart and let her out into life. It hardly seemed possible, but it happened. I heard it. I saw it.

I felt like I was with Jesus and Simon Peter, when Jesus looked at him and said, "I'm going to change your name to Cephas (Peter), the Rock. On you and your statement, I'm going to build my church." What a stunner! The other eleven guys had to be thinking, *Whaaaat?* They knew Peter as a leader, but he was moody and unreliable. Great intent but poor execution. "Stable like a rock" is not the descriptive language they would use. All through the gospel story, we see the unstable Simon. When Jesus is on trial, we see it in full force.

Jesus either saw something in Peter that he was calling out of him, or he saw a need that he filled by his words. Either way, through those words he gave Simon-soon-to-be-Peter hope and a future that day.

That is what affirming words do.

They fuel hope and give us a future.

12

Fighting Fair

If you actually succeed in creating a utopia,
you've created a world without conflict, in
which everything is perfect. And if there's no
conflict, there are no stories worth telling—or
reading!

—Veronica Roth

Y ou have to say 'I'm sorry' a hundred times fast before I'll let you
come downstairs!" Jenny said to Susanna.

Our daughters were six and three. Saying "I'm sorry" a hundred
times fast was a little kid's version of saying "rubber baby buggy bum-
pers." Impossible. When I asked Ruth, "Why do the kids scrap and
squabble so much?" she gave me one of those looks that said, "If you
would take the time to remember or perhaps to think in a straight line,
you'd know the answer to that question. They are kids."

We discover early that life is more than affirming words. In-your-
face stuff happens over things large and small, things of consequence
and no consequence. People see life from different angles. Everywhere
we turn, tensions flare around the globe. A cemetery may be the only
place devoid of conflict. As far as I know.

Every human relationship will involve conflict. If there is none, there is no stake, no investment. Each person brings his or her uniqueness to the table with feelings and ideas and passion. Differences pop up, but friendship finds a way to work through the differences to another good day.

Because I like to be liked, my tendency has always been to avoid conflict. Because I spent my teen years in a home where tension bubbled just beneath the surface, again my tendency is to avoid conflict. Because I'd rather love than fight, my tendency is to avoid conflict. I am not alone in this. There are many people just like me.

Resolution lies in this question: How do we see conflict? For much of my life I saw it as a negative because of how it made me feel. I was wrong in that assessment. It is neutral, neither good nor bad. My response to it makes it good or bad. Response takes conflict out of neutral and puts it in gear. The gear we select will move us either forward or backward. We get to choose.

David Augsburger, who served many years as a Mennonite pastor in Washington, DC, has some insightful thoughts on conflict. His book *Caring Enough to Confront* was pivotal in helping me see conflict and confrontation in a new light. He lists five ways we usually respond to conflict:

Of the five options in conflict situations—(1) I win—you lose; (2) I want out, I'll withdraw; (3) I'll give in for good relations; (4) I'll meet you halfway; (5) I can care and confront—the last is the most effective, the most truly loving, the most growth-promoting for human relationships. But often it will not be the starting point, but the long-term goal.[1]

I'll Get You

This response is the most visceral and natural. You confront me and I attack you. From the schoolyard to the boardroom, we know this action. You push me and I push back. Sometimes when we know a conflict is imminent, we can even make a preemptive strike. We say in our heads, *I'm right. You're wrong. And, I'm gonna get you.* We've all done it.

I'll Give In

This approach is a typical avoidance mechanism. "You're always right. I'm always wrong. I'll just curl up in the prenatal position over here on the floor and eat some worms." The person who always yields to the other to avoid conflict is not helping the relationship.

I'll Get Out

Nothing makes our point better, we think, than walking away. "If that's how you're going to be, I'm out!" We think that getting away from the offending party is the ultimate way to avoid discomfort. Actually, if the confrontation is intense, taking a break and stepping away temporarily may not be bad. But to get in the habit of leaving is of no help.

Let's Meet Halfway

Compromise is always promising. It means each party comes halfway toward the other. It eases tensions immediately.

I Care Enough to Confront

My tendency is to confront the person I have an issue with. But there has to be a better way to deal with a problem besides shouting, "Who's the idiot who left the Diet Pepsi on the end table in the family room?" When I do that, I assassinate someone's character for the sake of a watermark on the table.

In my view, caring and confronting in simplest form is affirming the person and confronting the issue. We see Jesus do this several times in the Gospels. John 13 and 14 record him engaging a some-guys-might-leave-you-but-I-never-will Simon Peter on the night before the Crucifixion:

> Peter asked, "Lord, why can't I follow you now? I will lay down my life for you."
>
> Then Jesus answered, "Will you really lay down your life for me? I tell you the truth, before the rooster crows, you will disown me three times![2]

He confronts the issue, then affirms all the disciples in the very next sentence:

> Do not let your hearts be troubled. Trust in God; trust also in me. In my Father's house are many rooms; if it were not so, I would have told you. I am going there to prepare a place for you. And if I go and prepare a place for you, I will come back and take you to be with me that you also may be where I am.[3]

My very favorite example is the passage that begins John 8. Sometimes contested because it's not found in early manuscripts of the Gospels, this passage speaks volumes about who Jesus is:

At dawn he appeared again in the temple courts, where all the people gathered around him, and he sat down to teach them. The teachers of the law and the Pharisees brought in a woman caught in adultery. They made her stand before the group and said to Jesus, "Teacher, this woman was caught in the act of adultery. In the Law Moses commanded us to stone such women. Now what do you say?" They were using this question as a trap, in order to have a basis for accusing him.

But Jesus bent down and started to write on the ground with his finger.[4]

We don't know what Jesus wrote in the dirt. It has been suggested it was names and addresses of women the accusers had been with. Whatever he wrote, after he finished he stood up and said, "Any of you who has never sinned, fire away. Hit her with the rocks!" He stooped down again to keep writing. As the crowd hushed, you hear the thud of rocks being dropped. When Jesus stood up a second time, the crowd was still there but the accusers were gone, their scattered rocks a mute testimony to their hypocrisy.

In my mind's eye, I see him reach over and tilt her chin up so she is looking straight up at him. Her face is a study in pain. The smudged kohl lining around her eyes tracks down her cheeks. Her eyes have the flat, dull look of someone used up and discarded. Then she hears his question: "Woman, where are they? Has no one condemned you?" (verse 10). She turns her head and sees no one holding a rock.

There has to be relief and wonderment in her voice because that simple fact takes her from death to life. "No one, sir," she says (verse 11). I see the broad smile spread across that tanned carpenter face, as he says, "Me neither. Go and don't do that anymore!" (see verse 12). Or to phrase it another way, "You are a great lady. And that's not what great ladies do!" And light sparks behind her eyes.

I don't know if the crowd cheered. But they should have. He was talking to them too.

VEGAS, HERE WE COME!

It was a warm California spring day as Dave Housholder and I drove the ninety miles inland from coastal Santa Cruz to Los Banos in the Central Valley. Dave had been a friend for some years since he finished his PhD at the University of Illinois with an emphasis on how people learn. He and his wife, Linda, had spent many years in South Asia, and their cross-cultural gifts were stellar. This was about to be one of those cross-cultural days.

One of our friends connected to Los Banos High School had asked me to come there to speak on building relationships in a time of conflict. The conflict at that moment happened to center on race. The farming community, numbering about ten thousand at the time, had a historic mix of Spanish, Portuguese, Basque, and white populations with smaller groups of Asian and African American students. The high school had seen some tension as the racial composition began to change. That week Dave had been visiting the college where I was president, so I asked him to come with me to Los Banos and bring a few of his friends.

On the way over Pacheco Pass, we were talking about his unique gift as a ventriloquist. I have never heard a better ventriloquist in my life and certainly never one that held a doctorate! I told him, "We're going into a setting that's a wee bit tense, and I need all your skills!" When he asked me how that might work, I explained Dr. Augsburger's five approaches to conflict. By the time we drove up to the high school, Dave was ready to go. His "friends" came along in the suitcase he carried into the classroom.

Atmosphere is a word that's hard to define. But it's easy to tell when it's tense. It was abundantly clear that the faculty and coaching staff, who were there for this in-service experience, would have given most anything to be someplace else at 4 p.m. on a Thursday afternoon on that lovely spring day.

The principal introduced me, but the atmosphere remained a stony silence. Choosing to address the elephant in the room, I said, "Well, it seems we have something in common: None of us really wants to be here at the moment." Then with something of a forced grin, I said, "So let's try to make it fun. I'd like you to welcome my friend David Housholder. He's here from Nepal. And he's brought some friends!" He stepped forward to halfhearted applause.

David proceeded to talk about the very different country where he'd been living for ten years, a country populated by very different people. Then he said, "I actually have brought one of them with me. Historically, he's been challenging to connect with and quite reclusive, but by great good fortune, we've become friends." Whereupon, he flipped open the clasps on the suitcase.

Before he could open it, a muffled voice said, "Hey! What's going on out there?"

David replied, "Well, I'm here with some new friends that I want you to meet."

"Oh, I don't know about that," the voice said. "What are they like?"

"Well, come see," David said, as he brought a large, green shaggy arm sock out of the suitcase.

"This fine fellow is my friend, the yeti!" We were looking at a bright-green cousin of Sesame Street's Cookie Monster.

"My friend, the yeti, is an abominable snowman. Quite rare and quite, shall we say, 'different?'" David continued.

"So how has it been, coming to America? How have you been received?"

"Well," the yeti said, "when I came to New York, when people saw me—all green and shaggy like this—children screamed and men tried to attack me!" (I'll get you!)

"Then when I got to Chicago, it was Christmas so I thought I'd try a different tack. Being green like I am, I hired on as a Christmas tree. But it is *so* tiring standing stock-still for hours on end with your head tilted back and a star on the end of your nose!" (I'll give in.)

A couple of the teachers chuckled.

"So how was it when you got out here to California?" David asked.

"Really interesting," the yeti said. "After all the judgment I'd felt in New York and the strain of Chicago, I was pretty anxious. But, you know, the greatest thing happened. I visited the University of California at Santa Cruz and *(pausing)* nobody even seemed to notice me!"

In that moment, the faculty from this quite conservative section of the state exploded in laughter. David had them. The coaches in the back row of the tiered classroom, who had expressed boredom by lighting up cigarettes and gazing absent-mindedly out the windows to their right, turned toward David and stubbed out their smokes. The older teacher, who had been thumbing through a book because she had been-here-done-this a hundred times before, closed her book and looked up.

David said, "So, what do you do when the pressure just builds up? How do you handle it?"

"Well," said the yeti, "when I really feel beat up and hurt and just can't take it anymore, I climb back in that suitcase with my other friends. Then we talk about how hard it is to do what we do, how unappreciated we are, and how nobody really understands how valuable we are!"

"What do you call that place?" David asked.

The yeti looked up at him, then out at the audience of about thirty teachers and said, "We call that the puppets' . . . (pause) *lounge*." (I'll get out.)

It was dead silent for two beats. Then the room erupted in cheers and applause.

At the end of the hour, the tension was gone and we had a new set of friends. The older female teacher walked up to David and paid him the highest of compliments: "I was in Vegas a few weeks ago and paid big money to see somebody who wasn't nearly as good as you. You've missed your calling!"

What might have become conflict piled onto other conflicts had become a window to resolution. And friends had been gained.

Friends can count on conflict.

And friends can count on resolving it.

13

Doing Good

Three things in human life are important: the first
is to be kind; the second is to be kind; and the
third is to be kind.

—Henry James

Talk only goes so far. What we want is action.

The apostle James echoed this sentiment in his letter to folks in the first-century church when he said, "Faith by itself, if it is not accompanied by action, is dead."[1] It's all well and good to pray for people and say affirming things, you say, but what are you *doing* for them? What's the concrete outworking of your thoughts and prayers? At some point, to affirm is to act.

One of the great things I love about Jesus is just that: *He is a doer.* He came, he died, he rose again, he unlocked doors, and he's coming back. As my friend Bob Goff says so succinctly, "Love does!" In the Gospels, Jesus does again and again and again. His patience with Simon Peter, this disciple who would have flunked the latest personality inventory, was a great encouragement.

Let's set the scene. Jesus will die within twenty-four hours and has asked his closest disciples to pray with him in the Garden of

Gethsemane for an hour the evening before. They fall asleep. Three times. Then the temple guards come for Jesus. Peter jumps to his feet, grabs his short sword, and takes a swing at the closest guy. Peter tries to defend God. Perhaps it's the sleep in his eyes or I-just-woke-up disorientation, but his aim is not so great. He cuts off the guy's ear instead of his head.

One can almost hear Jesus mutter "Oh, boy" under his breath. Then he acts. He does something to undo what Peter has done with his good heart and bad aim. I see Jesus reaching down and picking up the ear. Perhaps he cups it in the palm of his hand and presses it to the bloody hole on the side of the young man's face. Holding the servant's head in both his hands, he looks into his eyes and says, "Sorry. Now you're good." Then Jesus releases him to wholeness.

What an affirming act toward the servant and toward Peter. The last thing Peter needs is an attempted murder charge lodged against him by the high priest's people. Can you imagine the young man hauling Peter before the judge saying, "This big guy tried to kill me. It was pure luck that I still have my head, let alone my ear!"

The judge says, "So, *what* did he do?"

"Well, he cut my ear off!"

Really? Which one?

"Well *this* one!" he says, as he touches his right ear lobe.

"Looks perfectly fine to me!" says the judge. "Case dismissed for lack of evidence."[2]

End of story.

That, of course, is what Jesus does. He destroys the evidence. Try to prove in court Peter's action without the severed ear. No evidence. Try to say the Carpenter from Nazareth is still dead without having a body at hand. No evidence. At the end of time, when the Accuser says, "I know Foth. He's got a list of sins as big as all outdoors!" the Father will look at the list and say, "I see nothing here. This has Paid in Full stamped on it in the blood of my Son." Evidence destroyed. Now *that's* taking an action on your behalf!

Friends take action. They find ways to invest in you. They cheer when good happens. They weep when you are in pain. They figure out what you need and find a way to get it.

ON THE JOURNEY

In December of 1964, I was scrambling to finish a Master's thesis at Wheaton Graduate School. Newly married, we lived on Ruth's salary as a secretary, fifty dollars a week. My focus was Latin America and hardly any books had been written on my particular subject. What I needed was a primary resource: personal interviews.

At that time, every three years since 1946, Intervarsity Christian Fellowship had hosted a conference held the week between Christmas and New Year's on the campus of the University of Illinois in Urbana. It was an inspirational missions-oriented event for university students. More than two hundred mission groups and denominations would send representatives. The week was called simply the Urbana Conference.

One day my advisor, Dr. Lois LeBar, asked me if I was going to the Urbana Conference. I said, "I'd love to, Dr. Lois, but it costs fifty dollars for the week. Besides I'd never go without Ruth." At that, she stood and walked into the next room. Back in two minutes, she reached for my hand. Opening it, she laid five crisp, new twenty-dollar bills in my palm. Then she said, "Take Ruth and go to Urbana." That action toward us, those five new twenty-dollar bills, changed the trajectory of our entire lives. Two years later, we would move to Urbana to lead a congregation and experience twelve of the best years we have ever known!

IN THE CRUCIBLE

He wasn't a large man, but he had a large reach. Bill Aramony had been a power in the charitable world in the twenty years before we met. His creativity had taken United Way from a $400 million charity in 1970 to a $4 billion enterprise by 1992. That was the year that he was indicted and ultimately went to jail for six years and eight months.

When we met in 1993, he was in the middle of his court case. Day after day he would go to the Federal Courthouse in Alexandria, Virginia, to stand trial on the charges against him. During those months he was surrounded by some new friends who understood the power of presence in time of need. A number were high profile, like Congressman Tony Hall. Others like Fred Heyn walked faithfully behind the scenes to encourage Bill and his family. In his time of greatest humiliation, Bill had found a Friend and Redeemer in Jesus, and a cluster of new friends who acted like him.

When I first met Bill, I felt awkward about broaching *the subject*. He wasn't awkward in the slightest. He brought it up with this thought: "Dick, I may very well be convicted and have to spend time in prison. What folks need to understand is that I was in a personal prison before this, and now I'm free. I am freer than I have ever been in my life!"

He came to cherish the handful of brothers who would show up consistently—one or two at a time—at the courthouse. He never got past that kindness. He never got over it. He never wanted to. And when he went to prison, one or more of those friends phoned or wrote him every week for the entire six years. *That's* a kind act! *That's* an affirmation.

When he was released from prison, Bill spent the rest of his life advocating for people who could not advocate for themselves. He worked on justice issues, not the least of which was a huge one on the other side of the globe: the country of Sudan and the tragedy of Darfur. With people dying by the tens of thousands, Bill, with other key people, made eleven trips to that devastated land, sketched the outlines of a peace plan in a hotel lobby, and lived to see a peace agreement signed in May of 2006.

Affirmation has a long shelf life.

THE UNIVERSITY VOTE

In researching this book, I called my friend Pete Bullette at the University of Virginia (UVA) to ask a favor. UVA, founded by Thomas Jefferson, speaks its own language. The campus is the Grounds. You are not a freshman or a senior but rather a First Year or a Fourth Year. It is a historic place. Pete and his wife, Amy, lead Chi Alpha, one of the largest student groups on campus. These are bright young people with hot hearts and cool heads. More than six hundred of them, at this writing, are involved in small groups each week. They gather for a large-group meeting each week called Monday Night Live.

My request was for as many of the students who wished to finish this sentence: "A friend is a person who_____." I was delighted when

162 of them responded with candid and insightful thoughts. Forty-three of the respondents were very specific about a friend being someone who stays with you in the bad times. They said things like "loves you no matter what"; "stands by you in the bad times, smiles with you in the good times, and tells you when you're wrong"; and "is brutally honest when one is going down the wrong path, loving when one's heart is in pain, and always present when no one else is."

Too often when things get difficult, people around us leave. It's too painful or too awkward or just too much. There may be no clearer test for a real friendship than the down times. Look at your own life. Think of those times when you felt worthless or stupid or alone. Now think of the people, if you can, who just stayed with you. They believed in you when you didn't believe in yourself.

That single action gets imprinted on the soul. If you believe in me when I don't believe in myself, it's like Jesus giving me a new name or healing an ear when I am dumb enough to grab a sword under stress. Few things impact me more deeply than a friend taking an affirming action toward me in my worst moment!

Do you remember a moment like that? Who comes to mind? What happened? How did that become a life marker? Were you on the giving or receiving end? How does that moment reflect the person you are?

Hanging out with his friends the night before he died, Jesus distilled his dream for them: "My command is this: Love each other as I have loved you."[3] How had he loved them? At every turn he had affirmed them by actions that accepted where they were, but he wouldn't let them stay there. He took action to show them what they had been created for. He raised their sights to look at the eternal. He had spent three years *with* them. He had been *present.* And presence is not passive. It is active.

Anyone who has known grief knows the difference the presence of a friend makes. Our sister and brother-in-law mourned deeply the loss of one of their granddaughters a few years ago. She was an infant twin who died of sudden infant death syndrome (SIDS). As you would expect, scores of people reached out and offered help. Some came with words, and some came with presence. Our brother-in-law, Terry, made a keen observation: "You know, Dick, when you experience mind-numbing grief, hardly anything someone says can make it better. But a lot of things they say can make it worse." Words can rarely touch a deep grief. Presence might. Actions will.

When Jesus said to his guys, "Come pray with me in the garden for an hour," he was working through the front end of the greatest grief anyone would ever know. He wouldn't have their understanding, but at least he'd have their presence.

A softly snoring presence may on occasion be better than no presence at all.

14

Reaching Wide

"Children, do you have any fish?" They answered
him, "No." He said to them, "Cast the net on the
right side of the boat, and you will find some."

—Jesus of Nazareth, John 21:5–6, ESV

In earlier chapters we have said, "Don't start conversations by saying
'What do you do?'" Begin with "Where are you from originally?"
because it's a nonthreatening question. However, there comes a time
when "What's your line of work?" or "What makes you want to get up
in the morning?" is right on the money.

To say the Pentagon is imposing is an understatement of the first
order. This five-sided symbol of America's military power with its five
concentric rings sits on the Virginia side of the Potomac River directly across from the Jefferson Memorial. Built round-the-clock in
one year, 1941, it is a bulwark of concrete and steel that at the height
of World War II was designed to accommodate forty thousand people 24/7. During the Cold War it was Ground Zero for the first
ICBM rocket from the Soviet Union. On September 11, 2001, it took
a hit.

As I already mentioned, Admiral Vern Clark was there that day. He had been named chief of naval operations in July of 2000. He stood in a stellar line of admirals preceding him with names like Farragut, Nimitz, and Halsey. Responsibilities were enormous, but kind friend that he was, he made time one morning to allow me to bring four of my friends from California to see him.

As we chatted, I asked a spontaneous question, "Admiral, what is it that makes you want to get up in the morning?" He thought a moment and said, "I wake up every day knowing that I lead the most powerful navy ever to sail the Seven Seas." Pausing, he said, "And I want to make it better!"

At that moment, I once again realized that what we give our days to defines us in a way that nothing else does. We were made to "do." We are designed in the image of God, and no one is more productive than he is. We don't call him the Creator for nothing.

Beyond that, when you inquire about my world, in some intuitive way I begin to believe you might like me. You are asking me to elaborate on what I give my life to every day. I could be on an assembly line building computer components or cars. I could be a surgeon or an astronaut. I could be in sales or design. It makes not a whit of difference. When you say, "Tell me about your world," it offers the possibility of a friendship. When you want to see or experience what I do, friendship is almost guaranteed.

Jesus spent three years mentoring a dozen young guys, who by and large were men who worked with their hands. Palestine/Syria is an agrarian society where people harvest the fruit of the earth and the sea, and it has been since Abraham and Jacob walked the land. When

Jesus taught he used pictures they understood: wheat, grapes, figs, fish, and nets. His sun-darkened skin looked like theirs. His carpenter hands were like theirs. He knew hard labor and long hours. He was one of them.

GOING BACK

When Simon Peter blew it on the weekend of Jesus's crucifixion, he went back to what he knew: commercial fishing.

> After this Jesus revealed himself again to the disciples by the Sea of Tiberias, and he revealed himself in this way. Simon Peter, Thomas (called the Twin), Nathanael of Cana in Galilee, the sons of Zebedee, and two others of his disciples were together. Simon Peter said to them, "I am going fishing." They said to him, "We will go with you." They went out and got into the boat, but that night they caught nothing.[1]

It's one thing to go pole-and-line fishing with your buddies. That's what my Outer Banks long-net fisherman friend Charles Daniels calls "'ookin' it!" If you fish that way and catch nothing, you've at least had a fun day with friends. Grab chicken fried steak and a Dr. Pepper at a country eatery and you call it all good. But when you fish for a living and are out all night and catch nothing? Not good!

That's where Simon Peter and other runaway disciples found themselves. With a lightening sky over the Golan Heights and mist hanging low on the still waters between the boat and the shore, they heard someone calling. The man standing on the beach was barely visible.

> Just as day was breaking, Jesus stood on the shore; yet the disciples did not know that it was Jesus. Jesus said to them, "Children, do you have any fish?" They answered him, "No." He said to them, "Cast the net on the right side of the boat, and you will find some." So they cast it, and now they were not able to haul it in, because of the quantity of fish. That disciple whom Jesus loved therefore said to Peter, "It is the Lord!" When Simon Peter heard that it was the Lord, he put on his outer garment, for he was stripped for work, and threw himself into the sea. The other disciples came in the boat, dragging the net full of fish, for they were not far from the land, but about a hundred yards off.[2]

Jesus had come here three years before to call them away from their nets to a different kind of fishing. Now, not *sure* what is real, they go back to what they *think* is real, their nets. But it doesn't work. Then Jesus shows up.

John knows that voice. And Peter, desperate for redemption, plunges into the water and swims the length of a football field to reach it. Jesus had called them from their nets three years earlier to show them how to fish for men. He's here to call them one more time and jams their nets with big fish for emphasis!

What a friend he is! At the lowest point in their young lives, he comes into their workaday world and says, "Let me help you with that!" His action is seared in their memories forever. Years later, when old fisherman John remembers it, he says:

> We proclaim to you what we have seen and heard, so that you also may have fellowship with us. And our fellowship is with the Father and with his Son, Jesus Christ. We write this to make our joy complete.[3]

GETTING DOWN

Four children ages seven and under are enough to keep a parent busy. I was the pioneer and Ruth was the settler. I was out there every day exploring new territory, making new friends, and generally plowing new ground. Ruth, on the other hand, was trying to repair ground that four kids had plowed up! I walked into the house that day tired from my adventures and just spread-eagled myself facedown on the living room floor. Worn out.

Now, if you have teenagers, they see you lying there and go find mom, saying something like, "Dad has weirded out—you may want to check on him or call the EMTs." If, however, you have small kids, they simply jump on you. The giant has lain down. An adult to a preschooler is just that, a giant. And when he lies down, he is no longer a vertical power but a horizontal, nonthreatening, accessible presence. That's what God did at Bethlehem in Jesus. The Giant lay down so we wouldn't have to be afraid.

On that particular day, my kids and I roughhoused on the floor for a bit. Then they ran off to create more mischief somewhere else in the house. When they did, Ruth, who had been in the kitchen, came out and sat down by me on the couch. Then she snuggled up. I said with a grin, "Don't stop, but why are you snuggling?"

She said, "You played with the kids."

I said, "Well, they're my kids."

She said, "They're your kids when you come home, but they are my kids twenty-four hours a day. You're out there having business lunches, learning new things, and introducing people to Jesus. I'm here searching for our three-year-old, who has abandoned her clothes in the backyard by the kiddie pool. But, when you come home and play with the kids, you are saying to me that my world counts. You are saying I am a worthwhile person. You are telling me that where I invest my days is of great value." Then she paused and said, "When you play with the kids, what you're really doing is loving me!"

I wonder if that's what Jesus meant when he said, "By this all men you will know that you are my disciples, if you play with my kids." He actually said, ". . . if you love one another."[4]

Same difference.

COVENANTERS

In a Throwaway Culture,
Staying the Course
Stands Out

15

The Pledge

God didn't make a contract with us; God made a
covenant with us, and God wants our relationships
with one another to reflect that covenant.

Dr. Henri J. M. Nouwen, *Bread for the Journey:*
A Daybook of Wisdom and Faith

I t is enlistment day, and the cluster of young people stand at a semblance of attention. When told, they raise their right hands and repeat after the officer:

> I do solemnly swear that I will support and defend the
> Constitution of the United States against all enemies, foreign
> and domestic; that I will bear true faith and allegiance to the
> same; and that I will obey the orders of the President of the
> United States and the orders of the officers appointed over me,
> according to regulations and the Uniform Code of Military
> Justice. So help me God.[1]

That statement can be called a pledge of allegiance, an oath, or a promise. But at its heart, it is *covenant*, a word that has fallen out of fashion. That's unfortunate. *Covenant* carries a punch. *Covenant* suggests a depth of relationship that a contract culture doesn't quite grasp. The very idea has gotten lost along the way.

That's understandable. It is an ancient practice. Whole societies and cultures were built on covenant, not the least of which are the covenant communities of Scripture. In Old Testament Hebrew, the word *barît* (buh-reet) refers to any solemn agreements between parties. Barît became closely associated with Jewish ethnic identity when combined with the injunctions against intermarriage in Ezra. *Covenant* here began to denote something special about the Jewish people. Covenant in the New Testament, however, takes a different angle. In Greek, the word for covenant is *diathéké* (dia-they-kay) and carries the idea of a last will and testament. It denotes a promissory obligation yet to be fulfilled.

Ancient covenants were not simply ideas or symbols; they were rooted in action from their authorship to the rituals that ratified them. Any mutual agreement could be called a covenant, but one unique form was a suzerain covenant, in which a king makes a covenant with his subject. The covenants with Abraham and David were cast this way.[2] The king identifies himself and what he has already done. He then sets stipulations and outlines blessings and curses, if those stipulations are met or violated. You can hear a clear stipulation in Exodus 20:2–3, when Yahweh said to the Israelites:

> I am the LORD your God, who brought you out of
>   Egypt, out of the land of slavery.
> You shall have no other gods before me.

He then went on to give them the Ten Commandments. That moment at Sinai is the defining moment in Israel's history. Abraham Joshua Heschel put it this way:

> God gave his word to Israel, and Israel gave its word of honor to God.
>
> A pledge goes on for ever. . . .
>
> It is a moment that does not vanish; it is a moment that determines all other moments.
>
> "Remember His covenant for ever, the word which He pledged for a thousand generations" (1 Chronicles 16:15).
>
> Israel accepted the covenant: Israel gave its word of honor to stand by it.[3]

Although the covenants with Abraham and David were somewhat different from the covenant at Sinai, one thing is clear: *Yahweh wants the relationship to work.* It is all about his grace and the appropriate response is obedience. The Ten Commandments are there to show us how we function best. I can hear God saying, "This is what you are designed for. This is how not to let loneliness overtake you. Take the pledge."

More than a thousand years later, Jesus was asked the "What is the greatest commandment?" question. He distilled the ten down to two, saying, "All the Law and the Prophets hang on these two commandments" (Matthew 22:40). Then, at the Last Supper we hear Jesus say to His disciples, "This cup is the new covenant in my blood, which is poured out for you."[4] His words have the character of a royal agreement, a kingdom covenant.

The fact that the church has divided the Scriptures into two testaments indicates that "covenant" provides meaning and coherence to the whole. To study "covenant" is to focus on what is arguably the central concept of the entire Bible.[5] Covenants are how the world works. We may call them treaties or agreements or memoranda of understanding, but beneath them all is the idea of a pledge.

Having said all that, the question is, What does covenant have to do with friendship? When you tell me your story, I learn where and how to love you better. I begin to affirm you. As relationship grows, it is full of little agreements ("Let's meet for coffee!" or "How about a daytrip to the beach?") that build common experiences. Covenants grow from experiences like that.

And covenant is nurtured in three ways: *time, tenacity,* and *truth telling.*

RUTH'S THOUGHTS

To be together in life
    even though our paths may part.
To listen with our hearts
    and tell each other the truth.
To lend a helping hand
    When the journey is too much.
To end the day as friends,
    this is our covenant.

16

On the Clock

> "I wish it need not have happened in my time," said
> Frodo. "So do I," said Gandalf, "and so do all who live
> to see such times. But that is not for them to decide.
> All we have to decide is what to do with the time that
> is given us."
>
> J. R. R. Tolkien, *The Fellowship of the Ring*

Time is a commodity. It's a commodity that is traded in your head. Hear the verbs associated with the word *time*: *gained, wasted, spent, invested, squandered, managed, lost, appreciated, taken, given, utilized, shared, granted, allocated,* and fill in the blank with your own verb. What's great is that time is the big equalizer. We each have twenty-four hours to use. If a 70-year life span has 25,568 days, accounting for leap years, that computes to over 613,000 hours. Subtract 8 hours a day for sleep and you have about 407,000 hours to work with using any of the verbs just mentioned. The question is, Which verb?

Time is slippery as all get-out. It leaks through cracks and pinholes. It evaporates with the tick of the clock. In a day of a thousand distractions, how do we capture time to grow friendship? How do we allocate and invest time to build bonds and memories? Relationships don't happen with the tip of a hat or a hit-and-miss text stream. They develop because we give and take time.

I wonder if Malcolm Gladwell's 10,000 Hour Rule applies. In the stimulating book, *Outliers,* he speaks of people who master skills in music and math and technology. Studies conducted by neuroscientists showed that no matter the level of gifting no one rose to the top of the heap without investing 10,000 hours of practice. Whether it was Bill Joy, often called the Edison of the Internet, or the Beatles, who cut their musical eyeteeth playing six hours at a time night after night in clubs in Hamburg, Germany, the 10,000 hours was a constant, about 415 days.[1] I wonder if we could become friendship masters if we were willing to invest that much time in our relationships. What might be the payoff?

THE FIRST INVESTORS

Five men, one of them a household name in government circles, sat in an elegant room in northern Virginia. We had been talking about shaping forces in our lives and I asked, "So, who in your growing-up years left fingerprints on your soul in a positive way?" To a man they said either their mother or grandmother. Why? I think the answer is quite simple: *time* and *interest.* Mothers and grandmothers by and large take the time to care, to listen, to express affection. Their impact in the early years is enormous. Time and interest allow children to thrive—they know they matter to someone. In reality, every human being has the ability to choose to offer another person time and interest.

Little kids sure understand that. They don't have an accurate sense of time, of course. For them, the day-after-tomorrow might as well be next year. They don't have a clue about the kind of work their parents do. They don't perceive the nuance of relationship or the larger picture of life. The part they understand is love by time spent. Love by association. What they want to know is "When I see you next, can we play?"

Henri Nouwen, a wonderful scholar and mystic, wrote the book *In the Name of Jesus* about a unique friendship he formed after his academic career at Harvard and Yale. In those years, he served at L'Arche, a home for developmentally disabled adults in Montreal. It was there that Bill befriended him. They would sometimes travel to Henri's speaking engagements together, and on occasion, Bill would be introduced. In the epilogue, Nouwen related the time he took Bill to Washington, DC, to make a presentation "together." Bill's idea of "together" was much more concrete than Henri's, and the audience loved the winsome interaction between Bill and Henri.

Nouwen recalled their conversation on the trip back to Toronto:

"Henri, did you like our trip?" "Oh, yes," I answered, "It was a wonderful trip, and I am so glad you came with me." Bill looked at me attentively and then said, "And we did it together, didn't we?"

Then I realized the full truth of Jesus's words, "Where two or three meet in my Name, I am among them" (Matthew 18:20). Often I had wondered how much of what I had said would be remembered. Now it dawned on me that most likely much of what I said would not be long remembered, but that Bill and I doing it together would not easily be forgotten.[2]

In the Name of Jesus is a book on leadership. As Nouwen makes his case for what that leadership should look like, he calls for leaders to practice downward mobility, to walk with others in prayer, trust, and vulnerability.[3] That requires a huge investment of time.

Lack of time is the curse of our age. By *lack* I mean we unintentionally substitute what we *think* is important for what is *actually* important. It happens most clearly with how we structure our children's time. We are trying to do two things with our kids: protect and prepare. We live in a day when children are kidnapped off streets and seduced on the Internet. Parents want to save their children from those things and also help them compete in the real world. Downtime is often seen as wasted. But there are costs to endlessly stacked activities, as one high school teacher notes:

> Seeing things takes time. Seeing yourself takes time. Having
> a friend takes time. And it takes time to do things well. . . .
> These kids don't have time.[4]

I said earlier that time is the great equalizer because we each have the same amount. It is also the great nurturer. Time is soil from which creativity and innovation sprout. Without enough time and appropriate atmosphere, relationships cannot develop their powerful potential.

TIME INVESTED ALLOWS FRIENDSHIPS TO GROW

The question that had been asked at the conference hung like smoke in a still room: How do people get good time together? My response was way too cliché. For when I said, "Well, quantity of time is not the issue—what we really need is quality," Ruth interjected, "Give me quantity, and we'll work out the quality later!" Well, there you have it.

We simply give time to the things we consider important. If it is not on your calendar, written down, or stamped in your brain, it doesn't exist. Words are cheap. The calendar costs you.

I find it fascinating that in the most extraordinary mission in the history of humankind, the redemption and reconciliation of the world, Jesus took so much time to get it done. Thirty-three years. Really? Come on. He's God. He has created the universe. Makes water and land. Heals folks at the drop of a hat. Everything could have been dialed up in an instant. Instead, we have the whole human experience: *conception, labor, birth, growth, vocation, work, sweat, sadness, joy, injustice, and death.* God took the time to do what we do, to feel what we feel, to identify with our suffering. He invested the time to get to know us and let us get to know him. He took the time to become real to us—to be believable.

Time invested equals believable. Believable builds friendships.

So when you read the Gospels, it's not just Jesus's singular story. It is Jesus with his parents. It is Jesus with Peter, James, and John. Then Jesus with the Twelve. And there is the group of women, including Susanna, who followed and supported him. The personal interactions you read in the four accounts of his life—Matthew, Mark, Luke, and John—are varied and unique. Of the forty-nine personal conversations recorded that Jesus had with people, no two are alike. This is no cookie-cutter, one-size-fits-all deal. This is Designer stuff. His focus models relationship at its deepest and most real.

My friend Mark Batterson said, "Jesus spent three years hiking, camping, and fishing." That's a lot of time walking and talking in the open air. That's a lot of time frying fish over a campfire. Conversations that happen on dirt roads or hilly trails have their own terrain. Talking like that wanders off into side trails and down valleys. They stop at creeks to dangle feet in bubbling waters and remember boyhood adventures. Conversations at night under the canopy of Orion and the Milky Way elicit deeper and longer thoughts. Thoughts that call us to the cosmos and origins and to questions like, What part do I play in all of this creation?

Time spent resting in the shade of a spreading fig tree doesn't distinguish between small talk and big talk or shallow talk and deep talk; it follows the natural contours of life and weaves a fabric so tight that hardly anything can penetrate it. It's about dust and sweat under a hot Palestinian sun, punctuated by wading in the shallows of an inland sea with wind gusting in your face and the cry of gulls feasting on freshly caught fish. Relationship doesn't get better than that. And that kind of relationship takes time. Time is the seedbed for knowing.

For Jesus and the disciples, it was three years, day in and day out, where public teachings were the commas in the personal conversations and miracles now and again punctuated the mundane. I wonder if the disciples thought, when a little girl was raised from the dead or a withered arm was straightened, *That's our man! We're with him!* They must have.

Years later the apostle John clearly reflected those feelings when he wrote, "We saw him, we touched him, we beheld his glory!"[5] Unlike most history remembered, the memories of Jesus would never outshine the moment that created them. The memories could never be better than the power of his presence as they walked together.

When eternity intersected time in the person of Jesus, time suddenly had more meaning.

17

Truth Telling

To the Jews who had believed him, Jesus said,
"If you hold to my teaching, you are really my
disciples. Then you will know the truth, and the
truth will set you free."

—Jesus of Nazareth, John 8:31–32

A s the old contractor surveyed the interior wall, one of our maintenance fellows asked, "Is there anything we can do to help?"

A load-bearing wall in the Dining Commons of the college had been rebuilt during a renovation. We were trying to save money by using our regular maintenance crew. The guys were tremendous and hardworking generalists but not professional drywall installers. The twenty-foot-high interior wall's surface looked rather, shall we say, wavy. The seams were obvious. It was time for help from outside pros.

With a grin, the contractor, said, "No. I believe you fellas have helped me about as much as I can stand!" Over the next week, he and his crew made things right.

In construction, builders use a plumb line and a measuring tape to help get things right. By getting it right, we mean executing things based on correct information. The plumb line provides vertical accuracy, and the measuring tape tells us precise length. Without the plumb line and the measuring tape, designing and building would be guesswork.

"Measure twice, cut once" is the rule of thumb in carpentry. Precision is the name of the game, and accuracy in laying out a foundation or the distance between joists or the size of a window opening is critical to both the stability of a structure and its aesthetics. The plumb line allows for accurate vertical relationship to be established for the construction of the building. In building, your eyes can play tricks on you. Depending on the relative rise and fall of the surrounding terrain, what looks correct may not be so at all.

That's just like building a relationship. Being able to read where a relationship is in its growth trajectory can fool us too. Relationships built on partial information and inaccurate assessments are no relationships at all. That's why conversations are so crucial. They help us measure where we are and how we are doing. Without chats like that, we are left to guess what's up. In my experience, guessing goes more wrong than right. Quality investment of time and energy is critical to the outcome. There are no shortcuts.

I have a nephew in the trades. A few years back, while he and his cousin were building some bookcases in my home study, we were talking about the cost and time. He said, "Uncle Dick, we have a saying in construction: Fast, cheap, and good. Pick any two. If it's fast and good, it won't be cheap. If it's cheap and good, it won't be fast. And if it's fast and cheap, it won't be good!" Simply put, if you want your relationship to be good, it won't be fast and it won't be cheap. Lots of conversations and time spent together will be required to get the right orientation and assessments.

Bill Bryson, an expatriate American living in the Midlands of England, wrote a wonderful book titled *At Home*. It's a history of housing. It covers everything from huts to Prince Albert Hall in England. He goes into great detail to describe the evolution of indoor kitchens, toilets, the upstairs and downstairs of wealthy English homes, and the advent of hallways and porches. We won't go that far, but let's just consider how the building of a relationship is much like the construction of a house.

The way the house is oriented is critical. Which way the house faces, how the structure catches the sun, from which direction the prevailing winds blow, and the stability of the soil all need to be studied. A house can take a thousand different shapes. The desires of the owners and capacities of the builders all come into play in the process of drafting architectural plans. Once the style and orientation on the property are decided and construction starts, nothing is more critical than the exactness with which the foundation is laid out. If a measurement goes wrong there, the whole structure is affected. Getting the foundation right makes all the difference.

Truth is the foundation for any friendship. When you know the truth of my history, it helps to frame our unique friendship. All along the way, as commitment grows, healthy adjustments are dependent on our telling each other what is accurate to the best of our understanding.

If time and tenacity are the tracks on which covenant runs, truth is the locomotive. Covenants allow truth to be told. If I believe you will not run away, that you will not bail on me, I can afford to tell you the truth. If I think the truth will cause you to run, I cannot afford that. I will hold back. But truth is more than simple facts. Truth defines what is real.

Relationships are not courtroom trials, and shouting is not the order of the day. But truth simply shared is the basis for all friendships. That truth is expressed at three levels: the truth about what I know, the truth about what I think, and the truth about what I feel. In a friendship, all three levels are needed to have the complete picture. So how does that kind of truth telling work?

We see how it works in the Garden of Gethsemane with the crucifixion looming, when Jesus talks to his Father:

> They went to a place called Gethsemane, and Jesus said to his disciples, "Sit here while I pray." He took Peter, James, and John along with him, and he began to be deeply distressed and troubled. "My soul is overwhelmed with sorrow to the point of death," he said to them. "Stay here and keep watch."
>
> Going a little farther, he fell to the ground and prayed that if possible the hour might pass from him. "Abba, Father," he said, "everything is possible for you. Take this cup from me. Yet not what I will, but what you will."[1]

Jesus began his brief prayer to his Father with great affection by calling him Papa (Abba). Then he said what he *knew:* "Everything is possible for you." Next he said what he had been *feeling:* "Take this cup from me." Then he went on to state what he *thought:* "Yet not what I will, but what you will."

Conversations that tell the truth about what I know, think, and feel are covenant conversations. I don't naturally talk that way, but I continue to learn how to. It's the plumb line–ruler effect at work: that type of conversation gives us an accurate understanding of where we are. And, often, where we need to be.

I have had hundreds of chats with Ruth over our fifty-four years together, when I've heard her say something like this: "Dick, I *know* you think you have to take responsibility for all those matters, but I *think* you are spreading yourself way too thin. When I keep bringing the subject up, it *feels* like you just block me out. It makes me *feel* that you don't value what I say to you." When you add the natural difference in how men and women talk to each other, things can get dicey. We've observed over the years that men are often quick to say what they think and women are much better at saying what they feel. But when time is taken to explore what both parties know, feel, and think, we make progress.

Speaking this way telegraphs a desire to understand the other person and not to rely on assumptions. Relying on assumptions is futile, and we deceive ourselves when we assume. We don't value the other person when we assume. And in the end, assumption simply settles for less. We owe ourselves more than that.

Many years after I left the presidency of Bethany College, I received a letter from a former colleague. It was cordial but straightforward. In short, he recounted a shift in administrative staffing that I had made during our mutual tenures at the school that resulted in a de facto demotion for him. I scrambled a bit to remember the circumstances, but I finally did. The substance of his note said, "I *know* you didn't make the change out of malice. I *think* you were under great pressure and made a decision you thought was right at the moment. But what I *felt* was a great devaluing of me. I have held that feeling over these years, and I want to let it go." I responded in gratitude. What courage and grace it took for him to write that note. I already respected him, but he rose in my estimation as I read that letter. He embodied kingdom thinking when he stayed the course and he spoke the truth. To this day we are friends.

David Benner caught the broad sweep of truth telling in covenant when he said,

> In caring for me, my friends support my emotional, spiritual, intellectual and physical development. They do not want me to stay as I am. Rather, they seek my growth. They want me to become all I can be. . . . By daring to be honest with us, friends offer us invaluable opportunities for growth. They can help us penetrate our self-deceptions and cherished illusions.[2]

Tenacity and truth telling are the great catalysts for success in friendship. Tenacity says, "I'll never say 'quit'!" Truth telling says, "I'll not settle for less!" When those things meet, covenant blooms.

And when covenant blooms, everyone wins.

18

The Long Haul

But Ruth replied, "Don't urge me to leave you or to
turn back from you. Where you go I will go, and
where you stay I will stay. Your people will be my
people and your God my God."

—Ruth 1:16

I was whining, and it wasn't pretty.

At a pause in the conversation, my friend had said, "I am on you like ugly on an ape!" He had listened, eyes on me, as I poured out my frustration over the dynamics at the institution I was trying to lead. I told him that I just felt like leaving. Running. Getting out of Dodge.

Apart from the animal reference, I was touched by his intensity. He quietly said, "Well, you can certainly do that, but I'll hunt you down. I'll find you." Then came the "ugly on an ape" part. It wasn't that he wasn't busy. He was busier than I. But his eyes said, "I will give whatever time it requires to be your friend in this valley." His commitment to me and to our friendship was deeper than my dark mood. It was Hound-of-Heaven like. One never forgets that.

At issue here is commitment to another's well-being for the long haul. When we see a relationship where the baseline is "I'll never say

quit!" it's raw power. Nothing tests the tenacity of a committed relationship like sickness or tragedy. How often do you see a parent push-
ing a special wheelchair down a store aisle, and in the chair is a teenage
girl with cerebral palsy or a young man brain-damaged in a car wreck?
The time and commitment required for the care and feeding of that
child is enormous. But the parent made a commitment. I marvel at
that love and care.

We see that kind of love lived out all around us. None of us would
choose it out of hand. But if we were on the receiving end of the tenacity, we would have a whole different view. I watch a young wife help
her veteran husband from an SUV. She stands close as he takes small
steps on a prosthetic titanium leg. The covenant he had sworn to his
country took him to a place of death and destruction. He didn't die,
but he lost part of himself. The covenant she made to him at an altar
three years before keeps her close. And it ends up with not just the
wounded warrior taking small steps—they take small steps together.

Not long ago, I was asked what one quality was most helpful
among individuals in organizational teamwork. In my head, I ticked
off preferred competencies—vision, initiative, communication skills,
flexibility, listening, commitment to growth, and so on. Finally, I said,
"Follow through. Staying with it." In a flippant culture, where narcis-
sism wages war with commitment, the very idea of tenacity in a relationship takes it on the chin. Four magic words are the life's blood for
any true friendship. Those words are "I'll never say quit!"

The idea can be debated and dissected, but the truth remains:
many times relationships endure and grow *because they have to*. They
are forced to it. Given no options. A culture of convenience implicitly

decries that principle as heresy. The trinity of immediate pain relief, instant gratification, and self-expression sees tenacity in a relationship as archaic and not profitable. In truth, real friendship requires steadfast commitment. In the words of Lewis Smedes:

> We get to be best friends by a kind of grafting and a growing together as we learn to trust each other, feel safe with each other, understand each other, admire each other, maybe even envy each other, and simply expect each other to be there to do things we especially like to do together. We commit ourselves to each other in snippets, in all sorts of little ways, over a long haul.[1]

Looking back at the story of the Gracious Father (Prodigal Son), everything hinges on the father's willingness to stay with it. Without his tenacity, there is no forgiveness. There is no redemption and reconciliation. There is no hope. Tenacity keeps the ball in play. Tenacity lays the groundwork for every possibility. Tenacity is the hallmark of a whole new story.

The son will never forget that when he left, his dad stayed. When he was lost, the memory of his father's house found him. When he gave up on life, his father never gave up on him. That's the story he would tell his children and grandchildren about their grandfather and great-grandfather. This is not just the saga of the Forgiving One. This is the saga of the Tenacious One. You can't discourage him. You can't shake him off. You can't shake him loose.

Tenacity comes in a variety of flavors: childhood friends, parents, siblings, high school teammates, college roommates, and so on. The story I heard in Guaymas, Mexico, many years ago ranks at the top of the list of what tenacity looks like.

You don't just happen upon Guaymas, Mexico. You have to want to go there. Perched on the edge of the state of Sonora, the city sits on the Gulf of California. Christmas of 1965, we went there with a group of high school students to work with kids in the desperately poor barrios. The pastor of the local church we partnered with was a stocky, smiling fellow named Jose Garcia. He was full of joy and compassion. Not the same man, we came to find out, that he once was.

Jose Garcia was born in Tijuana, Mexico, and in his growing-up years he fell into bad company and worse trouble. At the age of nineteen, he was arrested in Los Angeles and charged with multiple counts of everything from armed robbery to kidnapping. He spent eleven years in California's penal system and ended up in San Quentin. His mother was a believer, a lover of Jesus. She was in no way wealthy, but she scrimped and saved her money so that once a year she could travel to visit Jose. On one visit, Jose asked her, "If your Jesus is so great, why doesn't he get me out of here?" Then he told her not to come again.

After eleven years the authorities deported him. They took him to the border and in so many words said, "If you ever come back here again, we will put you back in prison and throw away the key!" With nowhere to go and at the end of himself, he wandered the streets of Tijuana, finally stumbling into a little church. It was there that the tenacity of his mother and her Lord got him. He gave his life to Jesus and was transformed. That's the Jose I met in Guaymas. The tenacity of a love that would not be put off or pushed away got him.

Ten years after that meeting in Guaymas, Jose came for a visit to

Urbana, Illinois, where we lived at the time. He was excited to tell us about the halfway house he was building in Mexico, a place for paroled prisoners to find their feet and their way with Jesus at the center of the program. It was a place for second chances. It was a place where the people who helped you wouldn't quit.

He recounted to me an incident in Ensenada, Mexico, when he had been invited to participate in a television talk show along with a businessman and a psychiatrist. They wanted to talk with him about his new life and new work. When the cameras came on, the businessman instantly attacked Jose, saying, "Why don't you tell me about this God you can't see?" Then he pulled a comb from his pocket and said, "I need something I can touch and see, like this!"

Jose said, "My knees were knocking together under the table, as I thought, *Lord, how am I going to answer this man?* So, I just said, 'Mister, are you from around here?'

"He said, 'No!'

"I said, 'Do you know my story?'

"He said, 'No!'

"I said, 'You don't know me. Lots of years ago, I escaped from a jail two blocks down the street. I was a madman. They used to call me El Changa, the Ape. I spent eleven years in prison for doing some very bad things. But when I got out, I met some people that I thought were crazy. But they pursued me. They said I needed to trust Jesus. And finally, I said, "Why not? I've tried everything else." Jesus changed my life. The man you are talking to now is not the same man who shot a man and escaped from that jail down the street.' I looked at the man and said, "Mister, you want to see the love of God? You want to touch it?" Then I extended my arm and said, "Here! Touch me!'"

Tenacity grabs us. It carries the possibility of loyalty without obsession. In simplest terms, it says, "I'm not leaving. I'm staying close." Recently, my friend Bob Goff was passing through and called to see if I was free for lunch. I am almost always free for lunch! Especially with Bob, one of the most creative, thinking men I know. Always outside the box, he looks at things from new angles. As we talked, he mentioned that many folks had asked if he would hold them accountable as part of their friendship. Bob's thought was, *I just can't do that. I have neither the energy nor inclination to do that. But, what I will do is hold you close. That provides its own kind of accountability.* Staying close is at the heart of tenacity.

In 2013, northern Colorado suffered major damage from another flood of the Big Thompson River that flows from Rocky Mountain National Park down onto the high plains where Fort Collins, Windsor, Greeley, Ault, Eaton, and dozens of other smaller farming communities are located. The rescue of residents cut off by floodwaters in the mountains triggered the largest air rescue effort in the United States since Hurricane Katrina. The Red Cross designated Timberline Church in Fort Collins as headquarters. They had space and were willing to help lead the charge in caring for all the displaced families. Hour after hour Air National Guard Chinook helicopters landed on the north lawn of the church ferrying people to safety, more than one thousand in all. But it wasn't just people. It was extended family members, dogs and cats, by the dozens. People were sheltered *inside* the church, while their pets were fed and bedded down in cages in the *outside* courtyards. Loyalty. Devotion. Intensity. It was fascinating to see the reciprocity of caring.

One other dog story, if you will. Edinburgh, Scotland, is famous for a story of a dog and his owner that expresses devotion and tenacity in equal measure. The story began in 1850, when John Gray came to the city to be a gardener. Unable to find work, he joined the police force as a night watchman. To keep him company through the long nights, he would take his small Skye terrier named Bobby with him on his rounds. They became part of the living landscape of the city night after night for years.

John later contracted tuberculosis and died in the winter of 1858; he was buried in Greyfriars Kirkyard. What happened next became legend in the city. Bobby, the Skye terrier, would not leave his master's grave. Except for accepting midday meals from the kind people in the area, Bobby stayed there day and night with his master. The caretaker tried on many occasions to evict the dog, but to no avail. Finally, he provided the little dog with a shelter by the grave.

When the city passed an ordinance that all unlicensed dogs would be destroyed, the Lord Provost of Edinburgh, William Chambers, purchased a license for Bobby and had a collar engraved for the little dog. Until his death fourteen years later, the citizens cared for Bobby while he guarded his master's body. If you walk to Greyfriars Kirkyard today, you can't miss the statue that stands across the street. It is a sculpture of Bobby with these words inscribed on the base:

Greyfriars Bobby - died 14th January 1872 - aged 16 years.
Let his loyalty and devotion be a lesson to us all.[2]

There is something about loyalty that is intuitive in us. We know it's good. We need to give it and get it. Adolescents sure get it. Chap Clark in his seminal work on adolescents, *Hurt 2.0: Inside the World*

of Today's Teenagers, talks about the practice in high school of form-
ing groups called clusters. Loyalty is at the center of these close-knit
groups:

> A cluster is familial in that once it is formed, there is a strong
> implicit agreement to remain loyal and remain intimately
> and regularly connected to the members of the cluster. . . .
> Because a cluster is formed out of an internal need for safety
> and belonging, loyalty to those with whom one has chosen to
> align oneself has the highest value.[3]

What a picture. I love it! I wonder what stories those teenagers,
thirty years from now, will tell their children about the value of a tenacious loyalty?

Testimonies to tenacious loyalty inspire us to want to do better. In
the magnificent Old Testament story of Ruth and Naomi, both
women walk into an arena of uncertainty spawned by personal tragedy. But the love Ruth bears for her mother-in-law shows up in a powerfully tenacious moment. When I hear Ruth say to her mother-in-law,
"I am sticking with you. You lead, I'll follow. Your people are my
people. Where you die? That's where I want to die. Where you are
buried? Bury me there!" it makes the hair on the back of my neck
stand up. Her tenacity had a profound reward.

In God's great generosity, Ruth bore a son, Obed, who in time
became the grandfather of King David, the greatest king Israel would
ever know. And a thousand years after him, another in her line, Jesus
of Nazareth, would say something that sounds very much like Ruth's
words: "And behold, I am with you always, to the end of the age."[4]

19

The Chase

So the Word became human and made his home
among us. He was full of unfailing love and faithfulness.

—John 1:14, NLT

Everyone wants to be pursued. Pursuit affirms value.

When a corporate headhunter calls, we feel something akin to pride. When that young guy shows up at the door for the first date, it has the chance of being good. It's the step beyond the group gathering at the local exotic coffeehouse. You feel valued. In the broadest sense, deep friendship always has an element of pursuit connected with it. It is the desire for association, or as they say in the Midwest, the desire to be with—to come with, go with, hang with. As children we equate love with the desire of others to spend time with us. I don't think we ever get past that. For our purposes, we'll call it "the chase."

Across the range of relationships—parent-to-child, sibling-to-sibling, woman-to-woman, man-to-man, lover-to-lover—pursuit is essential. The chase should never cease. It might manifest now and again as an e-mail, letter, phone call, or visit. Or it may show up consistently, day after day, week after week. It is a cousin to tenacity and should never stop.

Jessie Yardy is now in her nineties. We met the Yardys, Paul and
Jessie, when they returned to Illinois, in the early 1970s, after many
years of medical missions in India. They had six great children and
three of them were teenagers. Paul and Jessie's expertise in family and
children matters quickly made them a hit among the young couples in
our congregation. In fact, the Yardys were so adept at childrearing that
we felt perfectly comfortable leaving our four young children with
them when Ruth and I went on a teaching trip to India in 1975. We
came back and the kids had been transformed: they made their beds
each morning before breakfast, each of the girls had hand-sewn an
apron, and other achievements! We said, "Boy, we'll never do that
again. Letting the kids stay in a disciplined, productive atmosphere like
that!" In reality, as you can imagine, it was a huge encouragement.

Chatting with Jessie one day, I asked her, "How did you handle
being in a tiny village in the jungles of Uttar Pradesh, while all six of
your children were in a boarding school fourteen hundred miles away?
How did you communicate?"

Smiling sweetly, she said, "I wrote each of them a personal letter
every weekday that they were gone. And Paul wrote them on the
weekends."

Stunned, I choked out, "Every day?"

She said, "Of course. If they were at home, I would have spoken to
them every day, wouldn't I?"

I sputtered, "Well . . . sure . . . naturally. Right!"

That little exchange detailed *the chase.* Right there. It is tenacity
in a stamped envelope. It's love showing up in the daily mail. It is ideas
and feelings on a page that can be read in the early dawn or by flash-
light under the covers after lights out. Who wouldn't want that?

When I was a ninth grader at Frick Junior High in Oakland, California, a young twentysomething youth worker befriended me. He would come every Friday for months to pick me up in his 1952 Plymouth and take me to play basketball. It isn't that I didn't have friends my age. I had a bunch. It wasn't that I didn't have other options. I did. What so impressed me was his willingness to hang out with me, a kid ten years his junior, in a critical year of my life. I didn't get the feeling that I was a project, just a young friend. I don't remember talking theology or girls. But I'm pretty sure food was involved along with sports. What I remember was him coming to *my* school and picking *me* up at 3:30 each Friday afternoon that year. That was *the chase*. It showed up in a green 1952 Plymouth. It was not weird. It was not dramatic. It was just good—a thing that happens between friends.

Some friendships are lifelong and deep. They are of a different order, so we don't have many. During our fifteen years in Washington, DC, I watched people selected for high office come to town. Often they brought close friends. At other times, they reached back for them. In a place of power, where one is *not sure* why so-and-so wants to be your friend, it's good to be able to reach back. In a place of power, where one is *quite sure* why so-and-so wants to be your friend, it's good to be able to reach back. There is a kinship built over decades that is built no other way.

No story in the Scriptures captures that kind of friendship quite like the story of Jonathan and David. Jonathan and David are young Israeli men. One is born to the palace and the other to a sheep farm. Both are warriors because these were tribal times and they were warrior peoples. By birth, Jonathan should be king after his father, Saul. But because Saul didn't listen to Yahweh, the prophet Samuel anoints

David, the youngest of the eight sons of Jesse, as the king-in-waiting. David has a warrior's heart and poet's mind. He is a shepherd boy, a protector of flocks, who on long Middle East nights puts words to music.

After David goes rock-to-forehead with the Philistine giant, Goliath, he and Jonathan become instant friends. They swear a lifelong oath to each other, which plays out in excruciating ways as Saul, jealous of David's successes in battles and life, tries repeatedly to kill him. When David marries Michal, Saul's youngest daughter, he and Jonathan become brothers-in-law. Their stories and traumas are recounted in great detail in 1 Samuel 18–31. What loyalty! What covenant! What tenacity! What chemistry! What a chase!

When Jonathan and Saul die together on the field of battle, David does what he has done all of his years: *he writes a song.* It is a song that haunts, a lamentation in honor of the two men who at one time had both loved him. As Saul's jealousy drove him to fits of fury and forays into madness, David cannot stay close. But he always stays close to his friend Jonathan. The wail of David's broken heart is captured in lines that three thousand years later resonate deep in anyone who has ever loved a good friend:

> Oh, how the mighty heroes have fallen in battle!
>   Jonathan lies dead on the hills.
> How I weep for you, my brother Jonathan!
>   Oh, how much I loved you!
> And your love for me was deep,
>   deeper than the love of women![1]

David decrees that all of Judah should learn this song. At the heart of his kingdom, he must want them to know that they have not just lost a leader. He wants them to feel the loss of a friend.

What did King David and Jessie Yardy know to be true? Deep feelings written down carry conversation to another level. They give substance to pursuit and a lasting quality to the chase.

When Jesus left his home to become the Hound of Heaven and call us his friends, he laid the groundwork for every chase to come. And by his Spirit and the hands of eight or nine men putting pen to parchment, we have the New Testament. The chase goes on.

What a chase!

What a reward!

What a friendship!

RUTH'S THOUGHTS

> The decline in letter writing constitutes a cultural
> shift so vast that in the future, historians may divide
> time not between B.C. and A.D. but between the eras
> when people wrote letters and when they did not.[2]

There are just a few things that I treasure. One of them is a little stack of letters bound together with a faded pink ribbon—musings and heartfelt thoughts from over fifty years ago. Letters to me from Dick while he was traveling with a college music group for the summer. The words in those crinkled pages remind me of our burgeoning friendship and our longing to be together again at the end of that tour. They bring to mind images of a GMC Suburban loaded with a string base, five students, and a college professor, adventuring on the back roads of the West. One of those letters is lost forever in the desert sands somewhere in Nevada, snatched by the wind from an open car window and tossed among tumbleweeds and cacti.

What is it about a personal letter that draws you? Maybe it's the surprise element of not knowing what is inside and your impatience to find out. Maybe it's because you can hold the letter in your hands and read and reread it and discover every nuance. Or maybe it's just the knowledge that someone is thinking of you.

I first learned the true value of letters when I moved away from home to attend college. A highlight of my day was going to the dorm lobby, opening my mailbox, and finding a letter from my folks. I would tuck it away, then find a private place to sit and soak in all the words and phrases that took me back there—home, with my family. I could feel the emotions of the moment when it was written, see my parents and hear them chuckling over something funny, and bask in their expressions of love. I felt connected.

When I was working full time to put Dick through grad school in Illinois, letters were just as important. We longed to hear all the news that connected us to our homes—sometimes it was good and sometimes heartbreaking. There was the day when we read the sad words written on paper—the news that

Dick's father was leaving his mother. We held each other and cried. And the day we learned that my parents and brother and sister would be with us for our first Christmas away from home. We held each other and laughed. In our little carriage apartment, letters were our lifeline across those many miles to the West Coast. Sometimes some cash would be enclosed, and then we made grand plans for the weekend—rent a TV, buy some extra groceries, invite friends over, and celebrate.

The urging to become more serious about writing letters myself began when Dick and I moved across the country in the summer of 1993. Our destination was the hills of Arlington, Virginia, and a cute Cape Cod rental on Vacation Lane. It was a new beginning in the midpoint of our lives, leaving a salaried position for one where we needed to raise our own support. The future was bright but also a little uncertain!

Dick was immediately busy with a lot of new, exciting opportunities. I had some time on my hands and decided to volunteer my secretarial skills with the international organization that welcomed us. Their values intrigued me. One value had to do with friends connecting with friends—either by visiting them, sending a friend to visit them, or by sending a letter. I began work by transferring a large list of those friends found on paper copies in a prayer book to a new computer system. In the process, I got to know the people who worked in the office—a real bonus. I was humbled by their love for Jesus and their selfless work behind the scenes.

Having finished my task, I was asked to join a couple of other ladies and begin writing letters to that list of friends I had just cataloged. Just a short, simple note with greetings, some encouraging words, an appropriate enclosure, and a friendly closing thought. I did have help—an index card system with particulars on our letter-writing history to each person and the guidance of the person who would sign the letter and add his own personal note at the bottom of the page. The agreement was that I would pray over each letter I wrote before mailing it. That became my privilege and day job for almost fourteen years.

It was a fascinating way to spend many hours. Never knowing just who I would be writing on a particular day was sometimes unnerving, but never boring. I had to laugh the day I was asked to write separate letters to all the members of a family *and* include one to the family dog! Sometimes I would phone Dick with cries for help: "Who is this person and what can I possibly say?!" I was surprised to find that, in prayer, God would often guide my thoughts so that I could meet the needs of those I was writing. When letters of response were shared with me or I was introduced to people I had written, I felt a part of a great network of friends.

Something I knew by personal experience was confirmed during those years: *you never know how a few heartfelt words on a piece of paper will affect the person who receives them.* Letter writing has something to do with vulnerability and thoughtfulness and a lot to do with intentionality. I like what Malcolm Jones said: "Writing a lot of letters will not turn you into Lincoln or Shakespeare, but if you do it enough, you begin to put your essential self on paper whether you mean to or not.

No other form of communication yet invented seems to encourage or support that revelatory intimacy."[3] And it's that intimacy that connects us across the room or across the miles.

When I retired from that position in Arlington and Dick and I moved back west, I decided to continue writing letters—just a few, to family and friends. If, for years, I had written mostly to people I didn't know, why not write to those I did know? First off, I thought of a few women who had been friends to me throughout my life—some whose husbands had died, who might like to find a personal letter in their mailbox each week. Then I thought it would be a fun way to interact with my daughters and daughter-in-law with a newsy note that included a favorite recipe and some "purse money." Later I thought it could be an interesting way to connect my fourteen grandchildren who live in three different states. I could give them our latest news, ask them questions about each other, add a scripture, ask a riddle or tell a joke, and tuck in a five dollar bill. The questions I posed would be answered in next month's letter. Once I began writing in earnest, I couldn't think of a more rewarding way to spend some time.

Personal letters are few and far between today because of our fast-paced lives and because we have other, more instantaneous means of being in touch. They have evolved from the only means of communication between people separated by distance, to being discounted by some as snail mail. The amount of time it takes to write a letter, mail it, and then wait for it to be delivered by post often does not fit into our schedules. The short messages we send electronically contain information, but unfortunately their purpose is not primarily to express our thoughts and emotions and how we live our lives. As such, they are often read one day and deleted the next. And they are in no way a substitute for a newsy letter that lets us know as much about the person who is writing as we do about their news.

It's interesting to note that much of our recorded history would be lost if people hadn't taken pen to paper and recorded the events of their days and their reactions to those events. We certainly wouldn't have most of the New Testament.

So join me. Think about some folk who might need your words of encouragement, and write some letters.

It's part of *the chase.*

DREAMERS

Dreams Fuel Hope

20

Trust Big and Dream Long

"What must we do, to be doing the works of God?"
Jesus answered them, "This is the work of God, that
you believe in him whom he has sent."

—Jesus of Nazareth, John 6:28–29, ESV

January 9, 1956, was a terrible morning. At least that's what I felt at thirteen.

The report had just come over the radio that five young missionaries had been speared to death the previous day by tribal people on the banks of the Curaray River deep in the Amazon rainforest in Ecuador. In the months that followed, they became symbols for devotion to Jesus for a generation of young people like me.

Women continued the mission. Jim Elliot's wife, Elisabeth, and Rachel, the sister of the pilot, Nate Saint, later went back into that area to reach the Huaorani Indians with the Good News. Elisabeth and her toddler daughter stayed a couple of years; Rachel stayed for forty years, and is buried there.

Elisabeth wrote several inspirational books like *Through Gates of Splendor* and *Shadow of the Almighty*. I read them all. So when I heard she would be available to speak in our college chapel, I was thrilled. After her very powerful chapel talk, she came to my office for coffee. During our conversation I asked the question, "What's the most important part of following Jesus, Elisabeth?" Without hesitation, she said, "Trust, Dick. What else is there?"

Walking with Jesus is a life of trust. So is walking with each other. In making the case for friendship, we have spoken of story, affirmation, and covenant as means and methods of making friendship a reality. The result of it all is trust and respect.

Reflect on that amorphous English word *love* one more time. In relationship, love is expressed through trust and respect. I have often encouraged couples to use that language for affirmation. Instead of saying, "I love you, baby!" why not say, "Let me tell you three reasons why I trust you"?

That's the place Jesus lands, when people who want to get life right ask him how to do it. The question "What must we do to do the works God requires?" is answered with "Believe in the one he has sent."[1] The root word in the New Testament for "belief," "trust," and "faith" is the same Greek noun *pistis*. That noun or some variation of the word is used more than 225 times in the New Testament. Where it is not used is in the gospel of John, which has as its purpose getting us to believe in Jesus (see 20:31). What John used is the verb *pisteu*. And he used that verb over one hundred times. All that to say, throughout the stories of Jesus and the apostles and the subsequent letters to those young churches, the thread of belief, faith, trust, and the journey of believing is the bedrock of it all. Trust is oxygen for their relationship with God.

TRUST IS OXYGEN FOR
EVERY RELATIONSHIP

When we tell each other our stories, over time trust begins to grow. That's you trusting me with your past and vice versa. When we affirm each other and start building covenants, we trust each other with our now. As we relax enough to share dreams, we trust each other with our tomorrow.

Trust, by definition, is a risk. On the eve of asking Ruth to marry me, I spoke with her father and told him of my fears that perhaps my parents' dysfunction was genetic. Sitting in the cab of his old pickup truck, he simply looked over and said, "Dick, just keep loving Ruthie and Jesus. I trust you." And the world shifted. To offer trust and be given trust are huge markers in our lives.

No passage in Scripture speaks of trust more intensely than Hebrews 11. The nouns *faith* and *trust* are used twenty-two times in thirty-nine verses. The great people of faith throughout biblical history are listed by name: Abel, Enoch, Noah, Abraham, Isaac, Jacob, Sarah, Joseph, Moses. And the roll call goes on with names like the prostitute Rahab, Gideon, Barak, Samson, Jephthah, David, Samuel, and the prophets. Wait! Was that Rahab, the prostitute? How did she get on the list? She was not the father of a nation or a rescuer of a people or an ark builder? She just hid a couple of Israeli spies overnight. What was that about? In that moment in time she trusted the word of the spies, and in doing so, trusted God. Trust happens at moments in time.

Just a couple of thoughts from Hebrews 11 as we look at Abraham and what God called him to do. He loads up his people, his animals, and his possessions, then he heads out:

> By faith Abraham obeyed when he was called to go out to a
> place that he was to receive as an inheritance. And he went
> out, not knowing where he was going.[2]

Abraham hears God and heads for a place he has never been. He's in the dark about his destination. And therein lies the lesson: *trust only works in the dark*. If you know where you are going, plans all in place with fallback options, you don't need to trust God. Our friendships are that kind of journey too. There is much we don't know, but we take it one step at a time.

The second thought is about Rahab. She didn't play on the big stage like Noah, Abraham, or Moses, but she played her part. She shows us that trust is doing what you can do, not what you can't. Most friendships and most of life are not about the big moments but about the hundreds of small ones. If it is true that genius is found in the infinite capacity for detail, friendships model that in a big way. Friendship is an accumulation of trust moments.

TRUST LOOKS FORWARD

Trust is a powerful engine for living. It produces energy and momentum in a way nothing else does. And though it exists in the present moment, it tilts us forward, encouraging hope and dreams. The writer of Hebrews actually started there in chapter 11:

Now faith is the assurance of things hoped for, the conviction
of things not seen.[3]

One of the best things about friendship is the joy of cheering on
the other person's dreams. When I trust you enough to share my
dreams, we have hit a new mark. You don't have to be the closest of
friends to share dreams, but those kinds of friendships make the affirmation so much more real. You might cheer friends on to check
items off their bucket list, the things they want to do before they die.
Or you might applaud them for an anti-bucket list, like our friends
Kent and Kay have. Their anti-bucket list consists of things they have
decided that they never have to do again!

DREAMS AND ACCOUNTABILITY

Dreaming out loud is a fun thing to do. When Ruth and I were young
and had small children, we played this game: "If you could build a
dream home anywhere in the world, where would you build it?" Having recently done a college retreat in Montana, I said, "Let's build a
home in the Gallatin Valley of southwest Montana. We'll be surrounded by mountains like the Bridger Range, the Tobacco Root, and
the Spanish Peaks. There's the East and West Gallatin Rivers that have
trout populations like nobody's business. We'll be in ranching country. And we'll build a home overlooking one of the rivers, with a sew-
ing room upstairs for your quilting endeavors next to my library where
I can write." And Ruth said, "What about schools for the kids?" And
I responded, "Well, we'll have the very best international school in the

world, just a pony ride from the house!" When you dream, you can dream anything you want and it's real.

Dreaming together brings one very special thing into play: *accountability*. Often we speak of accountability groups as a protective endeavor. In men's groups, it's a preventative mechanism, so guys won't get off track morally. But the accountability that comes when we share dreams is a very different dynamic.

Twenty-five plus years ago, I was leading a small-group exercise with some college students at the school where I served as president. We had just finished describing ourselves as animals and then describing each other that way in positive terms. The last question was, "If you had a dream, something you'd like to do in the future, what might it be?" When they came to me, I said, "You know, I speak at retreats quite often, and now and again someone will ask, 'Do you have those ideas written down anywhere?' and I say, 'No,' and then they say, 'You need to do that!' So somewhere down the road perhaps I'll try to write a book."

A few weeks later, one of the young women in the group saw me on campus and asked, "How's the book coming, President Foth?" Taken aback, I said, "Oh, just thinking about it." Then a few weeks after that, she saw me and asked again. This time I said, "I'm thinking of a title." That happened a number of times that spring. Five years later, Ruth and I finished a book on relational leadership.[4] And I thought of that casual encouragement. No matter how long it takes, no matter what gets in the way, dreams drive us. And friends can play a part.

That dream was tiny compared to other huge, almost insurmountable dreams we read about. Like the one nine university students and their coach had at the heart of the Great Depression. Nine ordinary young men from the University of Washington accomplished an extraordinary thing. They labored together in effort and accountability, as an embryonic rowing team, to take on much stronger rowing programs like Cal Berkeley and Harvard and Yale. And they won.

In his magnificent book *The Boys in the Boat*, Daniel James Brown describes what the boys' coach saw as they worked with and for each other:

> He . . . heard them declare their dreams and confess their
> shortcomings. . . . He learned to see hope where a boy thought
> there was no hope. . . . He observed the fragility of confidence
> and the redemptive power of trust.[5]

Brown details in exquisite language the grueling training schedules, early mornings and late nights, the lack of money, and the desire to quit. He examines the lives and the challenges of each of the young athletes and their years-long striving for victory. Then he tells what the coach discovered as nine friends fought for their dream:

> He came to understand how those almost mystical bonds of
> trust and affection, if nurtured correctly, might lift a crew
> above the ordinary sphere, transport it to a place where nine
> boys somehow became one thing—a thing that could not
> quite be defined, a thing that was so in tune with the water
> and the earth and the sky above that, as they rowed, effort was
> replaced by ecstasy. It was a rare thing, a sacred thing, a thing
> devoutly to be hoped for.[6]

In 1936, those nine young men took their rowing shell, the *Husky Clipper*, to Hitler's Germany to take on the world in the Olympics. And they brought home the gold.

Shared dreams push us to excel.

That is trusting big and dreaming long.

21

A Dream over Dinner

And he said to them, "I have earnestly desired to
eat this Passover with you before I suffer."

—Jesus of Nazareth, Luke 22:15, ESV

On the eve of the most pivotal weekend in human history, Jesus
wants to have dinner with his friends. But why?

There is no theme more central to the kingdom story, or your
story for that matter, than the idea of who gets invited to the table.
Unlike twenty-first-century Western culture, where food is grabbed
on the way to something else, Eastern culture just lands on the experience around the table. The word most often used is *hospitality*. It is
friendship centered in food and conversation. In the broadest sense,
hospitality is inviting someone into your space. It invites intimacy and
fosters friendship.

FOOD AS FOUNDATION

Eating in Eden begins the human saga and a meal in the Heavenly
City culminates it. From Moses and the manna to Elijah fed by ra-
vens, food is center stage. Every time you turn around, some food event

becomes a teachable moment. From Joseph in Egypt to Jesus in Bethany, we find ourselves sitting at the table. But why?

Eating is what humans do. From day one we eat to live. Beyond geopolitical, racial, or religious boundaries, eating makes us one. We may eat different foods, but we all eat. Being invited to a home for dinner has a closeness that a four-star restaurant cannot match. The place that gives us food for strength often gives us food for thought.

And so it is on the night before the Cross. It's quite a mealtime. Eat dinner. Break up a squabble between your followers. Wash their feet. Call out an imposter. Introduce the New Covenant. Drink to it. Give a lengthy teaching on love and unity. Be blunt about what's coming next. Close with a song. Go to a small prayer meeting outside the city in an olive grove. Get arrested. Go to jail. All in a night's work!

The three years of walking with Jesus's chosen friends is winding down. He's eaten hundreds of meals on the road and in homes with them. This is different. He knows what's coming. They haven't a clue. Five days ago, crowds cheered "Hosanna" and called him a king. Tomorrow, they'll be calling for his head.

What do you say when you know that before the sun sets tomorrow you'll be pinioned to a Roman cross? As you suffocate by inches, your blood will seep out of you, taking with it the sins of every man and woman who will ever live on earth. What do you say when you know the clock is ticking?

THE UNIQUE FAREWELL

I'll tell you what Jesus said: He told them one more time *what they were designed for and what makes life work.*

Scholars call the teaching his Farewell Discourse, words a person might say on a deathbed to those he loves. Though the evening featured a fight at the dinner table and high drama with Judas scurrying off to sell Jesus out, at the heart of the evening were his final thoughts. This is the ultimate "If This Were My Last Lecture" talk. He illustrated what he expected of them by washing their feet and talking about grapevines. But the phrase that hung in that room redolent with the smell of lamb and bitter herbs was "Love one another." How? "The way I have loved you."

The fulcrum on which his challenge rests for me is found in John's record:

> This is my commandment, that you love one another as I
> have loved you. Greater love has no one than this, that
> someone lay down his life for his friends. You are my friends
> if you do what I command you. No longer do I call you
> servants, for the servant does not know what his master is
> doing; but I have called you friends, for all that I have heard
> from my Father I have made known to you. You did not
> choose me, but I chose you and appointed you that you
> should go and bear fruit and that your fruit should abide, so
> that whatever you ask the Father in my name, he may give it
> to you. These things I command you, so that you will love
> one another.[1]

How fascinating is that? He doesn't ask, suggest, or beg. He commands. How can you command people to love?

I guess if you created them with the capacity and a will, you can.

If you've shown them a thousand times in a thousand ways in all of human history and, more precisely, over the last three years what love looks like, you can. If you've told them your story and affirmed them and walked with them in covenant and dreamed out loud with them, you can. If you are God Almighty, the Creator of Heaven and Earth, you can. If you are the Lion of Judah about to be slaughtered as the Lamb of God, you can.

We have said before in this book that the word *love* in Western culture is amorphous and used to describe many things with different intensities. Not so here. The word that Jesus used is *agape*, God's unconditional love. There are several words for love in Greek, another one of which is *phileo*, "friend." That's where he gets specific. The highest expression of that *agape* is that "someone lay down his life for his friends (*phileo*)." It's like he's saying, "Pay attention men. The laying down of your lives is what your future holds." But for whom does someone lay down his life? That's the question. He doesn't say "lay down your life for a spouse or a child or a parent." Those are the relationships that we would most readily describe as our closest ones. But he says that the *greatest* love is to lay down your life for your *friends*.

FRIENDSHIP AS A BASELINE FOR LIVING

Perhaps friendship is the baseline for any good relationship. I actually think that friendship is an atmosphere within which any real relationship grows. But Jesus is precise in what he means by it. He says that friendship is about sacrifice, which is easy to talk about but tough to do. Just ask Simon Peter. In this same conversation with Jesus, Peter had boasted that he would lay down his life for Jesus. Jesus, his Friend and Truth-Teller, in essence said, "Not right now you won't." In commanding us to love each other, he set the sacrificing of self for friends as the gold standard.

Although earlier Jesus took the servant's role and washed their feet, he made a distinction here: He said that friends are closer than servants because they have the inside scoop on their master's business. Servants going about their duties naturally overhear bits and pieces of the master's conversations, but friends are different. They are told everything directly, intentionally. But servants become friends when they are invited in. They have been extended hospitality.

They are not *serving* the guests anymore. They *are* the guests. He was very clear in his dinner talk that he had shared everything about the Father's heart and plans that they'd need to know. They were now friends who had the ear of the King, privy to the most important information there is to know about life. As friends, they would also serve. Just like their Master.

HOSPITALITY AND SACRIFICE

Catch the context here. Jesus is connecting hospitality ("Come on in!") with sacrifice ("Lay down your life!"). They would be intimately familiar with both practices. Theirs is a culture that is God-centered. Observant Jews go to temple daily. All day long they can hear the sounds of animals being sacrificed. Going home to eat, they often invite friends to join them—this practice is natural in Middle Eastern culture. And personal identity is wedded to the people with whom you eat. Jesus will die in a few hours in no small part for befriending the wrong people, eating at the wrong tables. He was vilified for being a friend of sinners. To follow Jesus is to give people your space and to give them your life all at one shot.

Throughout the evening at different moments, he emphasizes the importance of loving well. His point is clear: "By this will all men know that you follow me, that you love one another." Your distinguishing mark will not be that you love the world. It will not be that you love the great unwashed. It will not be that you love the down-and-outer or the up-and-outers. Your distinguishing mark is that you sacrifice for each other. When that happens, all those other folks will see real love. Jesus will show his eleven men by this time tomorrow night exactly what that kind of love looks like.

His Farewell Address has been meat for scholars and theologians for centuries. And well it should be. One could read it a hundred times and not fully wrap his mind around all the pieces and nuances. It helps me, however, to sense that in his final hours Jesus's main concern was for his friends. He wants them to get it right by standing strong and staying together in the face of all that was to come. And to end the evening, there is a song.

Friends and food are a natural combination. And now and again, at a birthday party or anniversary or just because folks like to sing together, music breaks out. Music and a meal are universal. All seven billion–plus people on the planet eat, and most all respond to a tune. Many actually sing or play instruments. You know how it is to pull up to a red light with your buddies or girlfriends in the car? You're sipping a coffee and your favorite station is on the radio. Loud! Suddenly, there's that great new song. The windows come down as the volume is cranked and you just start belting it out. Pity the older couple in the crosswalk. But they might just smile. Because they remember!

BRAIN TRUST

Eating and singing have something in common: when done in a group, the brain starts pulsing a hormone. Not just any old hormone. It is a very particular one called oxytocin, which elicits feelings of trust between people, a feeling of togetherness. Emotions, after all, are generated in the frontal lobe of the brain. The disciples had no clue about that, of course. The linguistic root of *hormone* means "to impel" or "set in motion." On that Passover night, once Judas was gone, moving toward trust was the desperate need. The eleven who remained had to be nervous. Feeling together would help. On that night, *together* would mean something that those eleven men from the countryside of Galilee would never forget.

In the Passover celebration, a song is a part of the meal. That song sung by Jesus and his followers would be the Hallel, Psalms 113 to 118. These are sung on feast days to remind Israel of Yahweh's love and provision for them. They are songs of praise for his character and actions. Look at the verbs in Psalm 113 that convey how they see Yahweh and what he does: He is *exalted* over all the nations, sits *enthroned* on high, *stoops down* to look on heaven and earth, *raises the poor* from the dust and needy from the ash heap, *seats them with princes,* and *settles the childless woman in her home* as a mother of children.

Jesus knew what his followers and comrades did not: *that, within hours, the ideas expressed in those action verbs would take on a transformed meaning.* In those hours, the Lion of Judah would become the Lamb of God, sacrificed to cleanse us from sin. No matter our station in life at birth, we would become royalty through that work.

Psalm 114 expresses the joy of rescue when the Israelites were freed from bondage in Egypt. Psalm 115 extols the love and faithfulness of a living, acting God, unlike the impotence of an idol made of wood or stone by the hands of man. The task, then, is to fully trust him and know the blessing that comes from that kind of trust.

ONE VOICE

As that impromptu men's chorus sang out Psalm 116, only Jesus would know the import of the words:

> I love the LORD, for he heard my voice;
>> he heard my cry for mercy.
> Because he turned his ear to me,
>> I will call on him as long as I live.

> The cords of death entangled me,
>> the anguish of the grave came upon me;
>> I was overcome by trouble and sorrow. (verses 1–3)

Psalm 117 is another call to praise:

> Praise the LORD, all you nations;
>> extol him, all you peoples.
> For great is his love toward us,
>> and the faithfulness of the LORD endures forever.
> Praise the LORD.

The crescendo of Psalm 118 carries the tag line "His love endures forever."

> Give thanks to the LORD, for he is good;
>> his love endures forever.

> Let Israel say:
>> "His love endures forever."
> Let the house of Aaron say:
>> "His love endures forever."
> Let those who fear the LORD say:
>> "His love endures forever." (verses 1–4)

Then a prophetic punch that would capture precisely what it means for "someone to lay down his life for a friend":

> The stone the builders rejected
>> has become the capstone;
> the LORD has done this,
>> and it is marvelous in our eyes.
> This is the day the LORD has made;
>> let us rejoice and be glad in it. (verses 22–24)

As the wind stirs the olive trees across the Brook Kidron, twelve voices join thousands in the same songs being sung in hundreds of other homes across the city. Rich Hebrew melody, some with marching cadence, pours out of windows into the spring night, flows down the narrow cobbled streets and washes up over the courtyards of the great temple. And Jerusalem, the ancient city of David, hears that song for the ages one more time:

You are my God, and I will give you thanks;
   you are my God, and I will exalt you.

Give thanks to the LORD, for he is good;
   his love endures forever. (verses 28–29)

And they went out from that place to another outside the city walls, a place called Gethsemane. That's where *together* would have its first test. What a story they would have to tell for the rest of their years. It would be *their* story, unique to that moment, but seen through eleven different lenses.

We know a little of that feeling ourselves in our own adventure called life, don't we? Because "my story and your story are all part of each other too, if only because we have sung together and prayed together and seen each other's faces so that we are at least a footnote at the bottom of each other's stories."[2]

When Jesus put out the invitation, "Let's eat together. I have some things to say to you," the disciples would get more than they bargained for. This would be no typical seder meal. This would be a Passover like none other they had known. This would go way beyond tradition. This night would transform them.

Little did they know that when their Best Friend began to speak, he would speak a dream over dinner.

And they would ride that dream for the rest of their lives.

22

When All Is Said and Done

> Friendship is born at that moment when
> one person says to another: "What! You
> too? I thought I was the only one."
>
> —C. S. Lewis

The telling of our stories is the entry point for every friendship we will ever have.

As we tell them, we remember our friends. They are some of the main characters. And in the telling of the story, those characters live again.

THE LAST REMEMBERING

Jesus of Nazareth died at the age of thirty-three. By today's reckoning, he was a Millennial. What a man! Accused by corrupt power brokers, he is condemned by a kangaroo court to death by crucifixion. Roman soldiers strip and spit on him, taunt and curse him, and rip his back with a cat-o'-nine-tails. Jamming a crude plait of Palestinian thorns into his scalp bursting the capillaries, they then toss a robe on him and shove him down narrow streets toward the killing place called Golgotha. Hear the jeers? Hear the shouts of bloodlust? Wasn't it just last night that the rhythmic sounds of the Hallel flowed here?

On that Golgotha hill, high up in the sight line of a watching world, he is pinned like a butterfly against the sky. Spikes through hands and feet, there he hangs. Shredded back with raked muscle, exposed ribs press into splintered wood. Relief only comes in the arching of his back to gulp air. He gets just enough to form some words. Just enough words to grant a request. Just enough grace in his long, slow dying to make friendship live. And he remembers.

Here, at the epicenter of the greatest story ever told, Jesus remembers. He remembers his Father's place, where he came from and where he is now going. He remembers his mother, Mary, the first face he ever saw on earth and perhaps the last one he will see as his eyes dim in death. He remembers his good friend John, to whom he entrusts the care of his mother. And, if you can believe it, in his dying agony, he makes a new friend, the penitent thief who asks to be remembered. Who wants to die unremembered?

In that remembering, there is redemption. *The One being executed for being a friend of sinners does it one more time.* The thief, guilty no doubt of many bad things, does a good thing at his moment of death. Unwittingly, he walks into life. He simply says, "Remember me. Remember me when you get where you're going."

But friendship goes beyond words, doesn't it? Friendship takes an action toward another person's world. Jesus does *that*. In my mind, I hear him say, teeth clenched against the pain, "Oh, I'll do more than remember you. Why don't you come along? Come with. Be with. Today you'll be with me in paradise!"

What an outrageous friend!

A REFLECTION

We live in the digital age, where *what we know* has been proffered as the thing that gives us life, makes us interesting, and gets us ahead. Some of that may be true. But in the process of gaining knowledge, we might lose wisdom. The thing that takes us wide cannot take us deep. In the end, *who* I know outweighs *what* I know a hundred times. It is in satisfying friendships that we find wholeness and, on the backstroke, happiness. The question is, How do we move that direction?

THINGS TO THINK ON

As we wrap up this book, just a handful of questions for you to reflect on:

What if friendship is the essential relationship for which I am designed?

What happens to my inner person if being alone with my digital device robs me of creative solitude?

What if, with all my achievements, at the end of my life I am really alone?

What adventure might begin if I asked someone, "Where are you from originally?"

What would it take for me to think through my story, to find its richness, and discover more of me?

What would it take this week for me to start a conversation?

How exciting might it be to hear another person's story and discover that I am in it?

How rich would it be at the end of my days to be able to name two or three people and say, "They are my friends"?

ONE LAST TIME

Friendship starts with story and ends with story. It is what we know. It is who we are. When we tell our stories in an authentic and vulnerable way, they become journals with Velcro markers to which others can connect. From our shared stories come affirmations and covenants and dreams. Perhaps best of all, our stories are the one place in our lives that we do not have to compete and we always get an A!

We do not need and are not able to walk with dozens of people closely. The God-man walked with twelve and was intimate with three. We should be so fortunate. He said, "Where two or three gather, I will be present." That two-or-three number just might be the most powerful number in the world!

So we encourage you to think small but to think deep. Think deep about God and man. And know if you do, your life will have meaning and wholeness and joy. A joy centered in a profound kind of knowing. If *to know and to be known* is at the core of our deepest friendships, that ancient troubadour is singing our song: "O LORD, you have searched me and you know me."[1] What a deal!

And so, on to the last question:

When all is said and done and you walk into the Father's house, what deep sense of belonging might you feel when he spies you across that infinitely crowded room and shouts?

"*I* know *you*."

"My friend! Welcome home!"

Acknowledgments

Without question, the greatest help in writing this book has come from our friend, Mark Batterson. Mark and Laura, in coming to Washington, DC, in the mid-1990s, brought unexpected pleasure and dimension to our lives. We count them as our own, whether they wish it or not!

Our deepest thanks, also, to the hundreds of young adults over the past five decades who fueled our observations by their questions and their friendship. Thank you for not thinking that we were too old to be your friends.

Thanks to all our friends of long years, who have shown us what love looks like through your gracious tenacity.

In the last twenty-five years, a number of small groups, formal and informal, have impacted how we see friendship: The Five Musketeers and Ruth's quilting friends and office buddies in Virginia, the Tuesday Hill Group who embraced Dick in DC, the Oregon Meethead couples (yes, that's the spelling!), our irregular Thursday Night Group and Ruth's quilting friends in Colorado, along with our present colleagues, Dary and Bonnie Northrop, and Jeff and Kay Lucas. And of special note are Kent and Kay Hotaling, who continue to model the truth that friendship centered in Jesus lies at the heart of the Kingdom.

Writing a book takes a lot of help. In particular, we thank Jeremy

Vallerand, Bob Seale, Tim Heist, and Justin and Mackenzie Matthews for their input on youth culture. Thanks also to Peter Hartwig II for his help in our biblical research and the support of Pete and Amy Bullette with the University of Virginia Chi Alpha group.

We are grateful to our editor, Kendall Davis at WaterBrook Multnomah, who championed the idea of a couple in their seventies writing a book that might appeal to a younger generation.

And finally, our deep thanks to The Fedd Agency, our agent, Esther, and the unflappable and insightful, Whitney Gossett, for leading the charge to get this work published, cheering us on, and being with us at every turn.

Notes

Introduction: What Really Matters

1. Chip Espinoza, Mick Ukleja, and Craig Rusch, *Managing the Millennials: Discover the Core Competencies for Managing Today's Workforce* (Hoboken, NJ: John Wiley & Sons, Inc, 2010), 14.
2. "Did You Know 3.0," YouTube video, posted by "cag caboolture," March 1, 2013, www.youtube.com/watch?v=JJEincCiGjs.
3. Sherry Turkle, *Reclaiming Conversation: The Power of Talk in a Digital Age* (New York: Penguin Press, 2015), 170–71.
4. Sherry Turkle, *Alone Together: Why We Expect More from Technology and Less from Each Other* (New York: Basic Books, 2011), 1.
5. Artistotle, quoted in Mark Vernon, *The Meaning of Friendship* (New York: Palgrave Macmillan, 2010), 123.

Chapter 1: The Great Alone

1. Dan Evon, "Pete Seeger Dead: Arlo Guthrie Pens Farewell Message on Facebook," SocialNewsDaily.com, January 28, 2014, http://socialnews daily.com/23194/pete-seeger-dead-arlo-guthrie-pens-farewell-message-on -facebook/.
2. Turkle, *Reclaiming Conversation,* 65.
3. Saul McLeod, "Bowlby's Attachment Theory," SimplyPsychology.com, 2007, www.simplypsychology.org/bowlby.html.
4. Leanne Payne, *The Healing Presence: Curing The Soul Through Union with Christ* (Grand Rapids, MI: Baker Books, 2004), 59.

Chapter 2: The Grand Design

1. Mark 15:34.
2. Luke 23:34.
3. Luke 23:43.
4. John 19:26–27.
5. Matthew 22:36–40.

6. Payne, *The Healing Presence*, 59.

7. John 13:35.

Chapter 3: What's a Friend?

1. Henri J. W. Nouwen, *The Road to Daybreak* (New York: Image Books, 1990), 64–66.

2. Robert Waldinger, "What Makes a Good Life?", TED, November 2015, www.ted.com/talks/robert_waldinger_what_makes_a_good_life _lessons_from_the_longest_study_on_happiness.

3. John 10:10, ESV.

Chapter 4: The Case for Conversation

1. Turkle, *Reclaiming Conversation*, 105.

2. Turkle, *Reclaiming Conversation*, 106–7.

3. Turkle, *Reclaiming Conversation*, 110.

4. Turkle, *Reclaiming Conversation*, 109–10.

5. Justin and Mackenzie Matthews, in conversation with the author.

6. Celeste Headlee, "10 Ways to Have a Better Conversation," TED, May 2015, www.ted.com/talks/celeste_headlee_10_ways_to_have_a_better _conversation.

Chapter 5: God, the Storyteller

1. John 15:12–15.

2. Luke 15:11–32.

3. "Meaning of Prodigal Son Parable," eProdigals, www.eprodigals.com.

4. Google, s.v. "prodigious," www.google.com/#q=prodigous.

5. Frederick Buechner, *Secrets in the Dark : A Life in Sermons,* (San Francisco: HarperCollins, 2006), 137.

6. NPR, "Remembering Pat Conroy, a Master Who Used His Tortured Life to Tell Stories, March 5, 2015. www.npr.org/2016/03/05/469337158 /remembering-pat-conroy-a-master-who-searched-out-the-world-in-stories

Chapter 6: Man, the Storyteller

1. Jeremy Hsu, "The Secrets of Storytelling: Why We Love a Good Yarn," *Scientific American,* August 1, 2008, *PragmaSynesi* (blog), https:// pragmasynesi.wordpress.com/2008/09/24/the-secrets-of-storytelling -why-we-love-a-good-yarn/.

2. Alex Haley, "My Furthest-Back Person—'The African,'" July 16, 1972, originally published in the *New York Times,* www.alex-haley.com /alex_haley_my_furthest_back_person_the_african.htm.

3. Haley, "My Furthest-Back Person."

4. Haley, "My Furthest-Back Person."

5. Paul Smith, *Lead with a Story: A Guide to Crafting Business Narratives that Captivate, Convince, and Inspire* (New York: AMACOM, 2012), 4.

6. Clarissa Pinkola Estés, quoted in AZ Quotes, www.drewgneiser.com/26 -quotes-about-storytelling/.

7. Smith, *Lead with a Story,* 11.

8. Philippians 3:4–7, ESV.

9. Brené Brown, *Rising Strong: The Reckoning. The Rumble. The Revolution.* (New York: Spiegel and Grau, 2015), 28.

10. Verla Jones, "Some History and Memories of the Early Days near Allan, Saskatchewan, Canada," typed notes given to family members.

11. "Homesteading," The Canadian Encyclopedia, www.thecanadian encyclopedia.ca/en/article/homesteading/.

Chapter 7: Your Starting Place

1. Daniel B. Allender, *To Be Told: God Invites You to Coauthor Your Future* (Colorado Springs, Colorado: WaterBrook Press, 2005), 2.

2. Allender, *To Be Told,* 3.

3. Genesis 3:8–10.

4. Oxford Living Dictionaries, s.v. "geography," https://en.oxforddictionaries .com/definition/geography.

5. Mark Batterson and Richard Foth with Susanna Foth Aughtmon, *A Trip Around the Sun: Turning Your Everyday Life into the Adventure of a Lifetime* (Grand Rapids, MI: Baker Books, 2015), 41.

Chapter 8: How to Read a Walking Book

1. 2 Chronicles 34:3, ESV.

2. 2 Chronicles 34:31, ESV.

3. 2 Chronicles 34:28, ESV.

4. Emily Dickinson, *The Collected Poems of Emily Dickinson* (New York: Barnes and Noble, 1993), 53.

5. Andy Rooney, *My War* (Public Affairs, 2008), 155.

6. Rudyard Kipling, *Animal Stories* (House of Stratus, 2001), 134.

7. Rick Bragg, *All Over but the Shoutin'* (New York: Pantheon Books, 1997), 3.

Chapter 9: A Journal and a Velcro Ribbon

1. Allender, *To Be Told,* 62.

2. Luke 2:1–7.

3. Pat Conroy, *Beach Music* (New York: Random House, 2011), 125.

4. Bruce Larson, *No Longer Strangers* (Waco, TX: Word Books, 1971), 35–36, (public domain).

5. Brown, *Rising Strong,* 6.

6. Frederick Buechner, quoted in Elaine Lawless, *Women Preaching Revolution* (University of Pennsylvania Press, 1996), 203.

Chapter 10: Speaking to God

1. Batterson and Foth, *Trip Around the Sun,* 185.

2. Luke 22:31–32, ESV.

3. Tony Blair, "Full Text of Tony Blair's Speech to the National Prayer Breakfast," Office of Tony Blair, February 5, 2009, www.tonyblairoffice .org/speeches/entry/full-text-of-tony-blairs-speech-to-the-national -prayer-breakfast/.

4. Philippians 3:10.

5. Philippians 1:3–11.

6. Ephesians 3:20, NKJV.

Chapter 11: Speaking to You

1. Carl Sandburg, "Primer Lesson," *The Complete Poems of Carl Sandburg* (New York: Houghton Mifflin Harcourt, 2003), 306.

2. John 10:27, ESV.

3. Philippians 1:7–8, ESV.

4. Batterson and Foth, *Trip Around the Sun,* 83.

Chapter 12: Fighting Fair

1. David Augsburger, *Caring Enough to Confront: How to Understand and Express Your Deepest Feelings Toward Others* (Grand Rapids, MI: Revell, 2014), 15–21.

2. John 13:37–38.

3. John 14:1–3.

4. John 8:2–6.

Chapter 13: Doing Good

1. James 2:17.

2. Gayle Erwin, author of *The Jesus Style,* personal conversation with the author.

3. John 15:12.

Chapter 14: Reaching Wide

1. John 21:1–3, ESV.

2. John 21:4–8, ESV.

3. 1 John 1:3–4.

4. John 13:35.

Chapter 15: The Pledge

1. "Oaths of Enlistment and Oaths of Office," www.history.army.mil/html /faq/oaths.html.

2. Walter C. Kaiser Jr., *Toward Old Testament Ethics* (Grand Rapids, MI: Zondervan Publishing Company, 1983), 76–78.

3. Abraham Joshua Heschel, *God in Search of Man: A Philosophy of Judaism* (New York: The Noonday Press—Farrar, Straus and Giroux, 1955), 214.

4. Luke 22:20.

5. Eerdman's Bible Dictionary, s.v. "covenant."

Chapter 16: On the Clock

1. Malcolm Gladwell, *Outliers: The Story of Success* (New York: Little, Brown, and Company, 2008), 35–68.

2. Henri Nouwen, *In the Name of Jesus: Reflections on Christian Leadership* (New York: The Crossroad Publishing Company, 1989), 100–101.

3. Nouwen, *In the Name of Jesus,* 92–93.

4. Turkle, *Reclaiming Conversation,* 71.

5. See 1 John 1:3.

Chapter 17: Truth Telling

1. Mark 14:32–36.

2. David G. Benner, *Sacred Companions* (Downers Grove, IL: IVP Books, 2002), 67–68, 104.

Chapter 18: The Long Haul

1. Lewis B. Smedes, *Caring and Commitment* (San Francisco: Harper & Row, 1989), 51.
2. Ben Johnson, "Greyfriars Bobby," Historic UK, www.historic-uk.com /HistoryUK/HistoryofScotland/Greyfriars-Bobby/.
3. Chap Clark, *Hurt 2.0: Inside the World of Today's Teenagers* (Grand Rapids, MI: Baker Academic, 2011), 66.
4. Matthew 28:20, esv.

Chapter 19: The Chase

1. 2 Samuel 1:25–26, nlt.
2. Malcolm Jones, "The History and Lost Art of Letter Writing," Newsweek.com, January 17, 2009, www.newsweek.com/history-and -lost-art-letter-writing-78365.
3. Jones, "The History and Lost Art of Letter Writing."

Chapter 20: Trust Big and Dream Long

1. See John 6:28.
2. Hebrews 11:8, esv.
3. Hebrews 11:1, esv.
4. Richard and Ruth Foth, *When the Giant Lies Down* (Victor Books, 1995).
5. Daniel James Brown, *The Boys in the Boat: Nine Americans and Their Epic Quest for Gold at the 1936 Berlin Olympics* (New York: Penguin Books, 2013), 48.
6. Brown, *The Boys in the Boat,* 48.

Chapter 21: A Dream over Dinner

1. John 15:12–17, esv.
2. Frederick Buechner, *Secrets in the Dark* (Zondervan, 2007), 137.

Chapter 22: When All Is Said and Done

1. Psalm 139:1.